"...With a hey ho
the wind
and
the rain..."

*Janet & Louise —
With love & happy memories —
with new ones to come!
Maggie.*

"With a hey ho the wind and the rain..."

A Personal Memoir of the Scottish Highlands

Tim and Maggie Shields

With illustrations by Jean Dinsdale-Young

Copyright © 2014 Tim and Maggie Shields

The moral right of the author has been asserted.

Apart from any fair dealing for the purposes of research or private study, or criticism or review, as permitted under the Copyright, Designs and Patents Act 1988, this publication may only be reproduced, stored or transmitted, in any form or by any means, with the prior permission in writing of the publishers, or in the case of reprographic reproduction in accordance with the terms of licences issued by the Copyright Licensing Agency. Enquiries concerning reproduction outside those terms should be sent to the publishers.

Matador
9 Priory Business Park
Kibworth Beauchamp
Leicestershire LE8 0RX, UK
Tel: (+44) 116 279 2299
Fax: (+44) 116 279 2277
Email: books@troubador.co.uk
Web: www.troubador.co.uk/matador

ISBN 978 1783064 410

British Library Cataloguing in Publication Data.
A catalogue record for this book is available from the British Library.

Typeset in Aldine401 BT Roman by Troubador Publishing Ltd

Matador is an imprint of Troubador Publishing Ltd

To Tim, and all our friends in the glen, especially Deborah, George and Marie.

My thanks to Jean Dinsdale-Young for supplying the illustrations and especially to Catherine Sauzier for taking my rough text version in hand and organizing it with such friendly and professional attention.

The Glen

It starts and ends with the landscape: the rocks, the incessant sound of water, the brushed heather with its wiry roots, the bent grasses, the pressed shapes. Minds that dwell in that land are moulded and crevassed by it and take their rhythms from it. [Tim]

Contents

IN THE BEGINNING	1
HOW TO CHANGE YOUR LIFE – A PROLOGUE IN FIVE SHORT SCENES	3
REFLECTIVE INTERLUDE	9
THE PROMISED LAND	11
The Long March	11
A Tour of 'Home'	16
Domestic Science	19
Landscape	23
The Lodge	25
The Estate	32
INTERLUDE 2: A GUIDE TO DEER AND THE STALKER'S DUTIES	41
SETTLING IN	45
Ponies	45
Goats	51
Roddie and Peter	58
Cow	61
The Garden	69
Pigs	71
Shopping	80
INTERLUDE 3: WEATHER	83

VISIONARIES AND DREAMERS	89
Church	89
The James'	93
Richie	100
Tony and Miranda	101
Ted and Jean	104
ENDINGS	109
Crack-up	109
Tim's Last Stalk	109

In the Beginning...

Tim and I were a conventional couple in our thirties when in 1974 we left our comfortable and secure existence in the south of England for a remote cottage in the wilds of the Scottish Highlands. We had no experience of rural life and virtually no money. But – in tune with the times – we had a dream. As aspiring writer and weaver, we craved creative space free from the drudgery and conformity of our present lives and a future of more of the same. We were looking for a way out and were euphoric when a challenging offer came our way – a part-time job on a deer estate, with house, in the N.W. Highlands of Scotland: time and opportunity to follow our creative bent, to establish a self-sufficient life-style, to discover a new world.

This is the story of how the dream turned out in actuality. There were many hard knocks and disappointments, but we did discover – for us – a new world, one full of wonders and an enrichment of life beyond our early visions. It proved an adventure in every meaning of that term. It was indeed 'a risky undertaking of unknown outcome'; it was 'a leap in the dark'. Even in our escapist illusions, we realised from the start that we were going to have to cope with entirely new demands on our physical and emotional resources, that we were going to have to learn to adapt in unimaginable ways in order to survive: this was going to be a trial, a test of ourselves, a quest, an odyssey. This was the challenge, could we rise to it and – in the original meaning of 'adventure' – arrive?

The answer to that question will unfold in the following pages, and of course the answer is not simple. In time, Tim, the writer, turned his attention to recording the experiences and impressions he encountered. His journals and notes provide much of the

In the Beginning

material here; it has been added to by me, the erstwhile weaver. I have woven our versions into what I hope is a richly-patterned fabric, but there is considerable variation in the texture. My main narrative account is interlaced with some sections that remain as Tim wrote them, and I have also inserted extracts from my diaries of the time. Tim's episodes have a detached impersonal tone which contrasts with the immediacy and informality of the diary extracts, but as I feel these differing voices add to the interest of the piece I have not aimed at consistent organisation and you will find a patchwork of styles and approaches. Whether this makes for interesting reading only you, the reader, can judge!

How to Change Your Life –

A Prologue in Five Short Scenes

SCENE ONE

It was his observant wife who noticed the advertisement lurking in 'The Times'. 'Couple required… ' etc.

'I'm not sure I want to work for some absentee landlord,' he said, leaning back adopting a moral tone.

So it was she who sent in their letter of application, and a few days later they were surprised to receive a phone call arranging an interview.

SCENE TWO

On the day set Tim happened to attend a lunch party at a local wine merchant's. The vintner was hoping to drum up business with the hotel for which he worked. The other guests were the wine committee from a nearby university, purchasing on behalf of their Senior Common Room. The food was excellent, the wines were various. After the meal, the party was conducted on a tour of the cellars where further wines were sampled. The afternoon passed in a sort of buoyant mist. When eventually he found himself back on the street, blinking against the low-slung sun, Tim realised that the time of the interview was approaching and his mind was hardly focused. So he strode out along the beach, the uncooperative pebbles shifting and grinding underfoot. He walked and walked, scrambling over the mighty groynes in his best grey waistcoated suit, hoping the sea breezes would clear away those curling fumes. By the time he had travelled several groynes heading westwards and the same number of groynes returning eastwards to where he had left the car, he was well behind schedule. But at least things had stopped rocking. He drove off smartly, heading north. About halfway to the destination a back tyre punctured.

The large gabled house was in a village about twelve miles out of the town. The front door was opened by the Captain himself. He gave a suspicious scowl of welcome that augured well for future relations.

I had already arrived and was making polite conversation. I looked anxiously at Tim's oily hands and general disarray, but no-one else seemed bothered. The Captain wasted no time on small talk, but began describing what the job entailed, producing maps and photographs of the estate. The photographs showed little but brown hills and water.

'It does look lovely,' I ventured hesitantly.

'The pictures don't really show how steep the hills are,' the Captain's wife said. She had a tired, gentle face, and sat on the arm of the settee in her overcoat. She toned in tastefully with the pale green décor.

'You can see better if you look at the map,' the Captain barked. 'You can read a map? You see the contours are very close together all the way down the lochside.'

Yes, Tim noticed, they were very close together. They also seemed to be in constant motion. He was reminded of once looking into a fisherman's tin of wriggling worm bait. He felt the feathery touch of nausea, but it passed.

They were offered tea or sherry and chose tea.

It was suggested that as they were already planning a trip to Skye over Easter, they might care to visit the estate in passing.

'It is beautiful,' the Captain said, 'but it's pretty remote up there. It would be best for you to see what you're letting yourselves in for.'

SCENE THREE

There is a photograph taken on that Easter visit, a rear view of Tim wearing a tattered old parachutist's jacket and wielding a stick, standing on the path and surveying the wide, flat plateau that constitutes the centre of the estate. Grey rock, blue sky, brown tundra. On the back of the picture is written: the prophet goes forth into the wilderness.

SCENE FOUR

The next interview took place a few weeks later in a terraced house in Paddington. Again we were late for the appointment. The Captain was standing in the portico of the house, wearing a tweed cap and his faded Barbour jacket. We mumbled apologies and excuses, which he disregarded, and followed him up the stairs into the first floor flat. The three of us sat down in the cluttered sitting room and for nearly an hour we answered personal questions about families, religion [or lack of], political affiliations, financial position. Some of these questions might have been thought scarcely pertinent to the job under discussion, religious beliefs did not seem to have much bearing on the repair of ditches, or politics on the maintenance of a generator. However, we tried to answer in tones which suggested friendliness, respect, candour, reserve and competence all at the same time. We wanted to reassure but not give overmuch away. As the Captain was rather deaf, we found ourselves having to repeat details of our personal history loud enough to carry throughout the building, if not the length of the terrace.

'And what are your politics, do you say?'

'Oh, sort of middle of the road, you know. Nothing very specific.'

[I noticed the book sticking out of Tim's pocket – The Anarchist Reader. I pushed it surreptitiously out of sight.]

'And are you all right for money?'

'Oh yes.' [God, no.]

'Of course it's not a full-time job. You think you can manage?'

'Oh yes.' [Gulp.]

'Your family will help you, will they?'

'I'm sure we'll manage.' [Ever hopeful.]

'What?'

'WE'LL MANAGE.'

'Good, good. That's all right then.'

Gradually the conversation grew more relaxed, and without any specific announcement of the fact, a decision seemed to have been tacitly taken. We moved imperceptibly from 'if' to 'when' and 'how'. In that hour, in that room with its characterless jumble, with the rainy late afternoon light making it seem gloomier than it really was, we realised that what had started as a casual idea – 'What the hell? Why not?' – had turned into a positive commitment. We had agreed to exchange, three months hence, our present cosy south coast existence with its obsessive lawns and elderly population, for the wildness of a Scottish fjord over six hundred miles to the north, where herds of deer came down to drink at night and the annual rainfall was around 120 inches.

SCENE FIVE

The property market was sluggish. Our house had been up for sale for three months with hardly a flicker of interest.

On Tim's desk were books of socialist economics – Marx, The

Paris Commume, Kropotkin's autobiography – strivings towards the equitable society. On the other side of his desk, estate agent's handouts, solicitor's letters, bank statements, showing that the primary concern at that moment was to keep ahead of the game, to salvage what capital we might have managed – thanks to the vagaries of the property market – to accumulate. We were going to have to drop the asking price for the house below what we had paid for it. But while the mind worked to adjust itself to the prospect of financial loss, it also built up reasons for believing such a loss to be salutary. If we were going to make the break to a new life, then surely it should be clean and careless? Don't get stuck in the mire of materialism and petty calculation.

Tim rang the estate agent and asked him to hold the current price for another two weeks. You never know, after all…

CURTAIN

Reflective Interlude

It is pleasant to think that we direct our lives by acts of choice, by asserting the will. But most of the time one just re-acts, bouncing off surfaces that one finds uncomfortable. We provide ourselves with convincing reasons for moving this way or that, preferring to forget that our prime reason is often the desire just to get out from under, away from wherever we happen to be. So it was with us. Though we were attracted by those hazy snaps of wild scenery, we had no real perception of what life would be like there. It did not matter. We were interested in visions not facts, and we wanted an exit visa from the smug, crusted environment in which we felt trapped. We disliked our jobs, our routine, our society, our prospects. Almost anything would be preferable.

We looked to 'the Highlands' as a place where we would be able to try out some of our cherished ideas. [Being 'intellectuals', we could do nothing without an Idea.] We would engage in our chosen crafts. We would experiment with notions of self-sufficiency. We would live deep in unspoilt country, away from the blights of contemporary civilisation – noise, dirt, engines, television, parking meters – the list of tribulations for sensitive intellects is endless. We would quote Thoreau's desire – 'to live deliberately, to front only the essential facts of life, and see if [we] could not learn what it had to teach, and not, when [we] came to die, discover that [we] had not lived' – and believe that it applied to us equally. We could pride ourselves that we were yet brave and resourceful enough to say Yes rather than No to unexpected opportunities that life offered… etc.

But in fact our deepest desire was – flight. The Great Escape.

The Promised Land

The Long March

We decided to move ourselves and our belongings. This entailed hiring a van in the south, loading and driving it all the way up in two days, unloading, driving it back over two more days, and then driving up once more in the car. Financially, it was the most economical way; physically, it fairly drained our resources. We had to drive through the deadening centre of the summer's heatwave. Temperatures were pushing into the nineties.

Tim went to collect the hired van. The mechanic apologised for its dents and dilapidations.

'But are you sure it will get me there?'

'Where are you going?'

'Right up to Scotland.'

'I should think so.' [Not giving a damn.]

Thus reassured, Tim drove it to the nearest garage to fill up with fuel. Still unsure of its width, he eased it most carefully in beside the pumps. There was a grinding and shattering of glass as the roof of the van accounted for the tubular bulb and fittings under the garage awning. Almost at once, a girl appeared from the office with a dustpan and broom.

'Don't worry,' she said. 'It often happens. Just leave your name and address. I don't expect you'll hear any more about it. By the way, we don't have diesel.'

The neatly typed bill arrived two days later.

We loaded the van and set off. Inside the cab, the heat and noise were terrific. Our clothes were soon wringing wet, sticking to skin, sticking to seats. We bought iced beer which was lukewarm before we got to drink it. Talk soon died out as the clatter of the engine took over, and our throats became prickly. The weight of furniture behind us caused the truck to lurch left and right with a sickening motion. Distance was measured by filling stations.

So:

Several hundred miles driven south to north up the length of the country's spine, plus eight leagues down a one-track road, its passing places sprinkled with deer pellets, turning right over a faded red wooden bridge whose loose timbers rattled like a dud marimba, slaloming down the unmade drive, squirting pebbles out of the dried puddle holes, passing between iron gate posts which held up a few derelict strands of wire, bearing right between triffid-like tendrils of rhododendron – delivered us into another world: an unimaginable, unforeseeable way of living. Its initial markers, a large black shed with raw-cut fencing posts leaning against its side wall, then a little to the left, the low-stretched cottage with its orange front door, the white-washed façade of the living quarters giving way to rough mottled stonework at the stable end.

A still, close evening in August, when the sun has gone and there is no breeze to stir the moistening air, is the very favourite atmosphere for midges. A welcoming flotilla hung around the cottage, smelling out dinner. As part of our efficient packing system, we had put the bed to the front of the van to act as cushioning, but now it was the first thing we wanted to get out. As we delved into the darkening interior, the midges swarmed in after us, attacking any millimetre of exposed flesh. We tore at ropes, flung aside chairs, lamps, cushions in our frantic haste to reach that damn bed, flailing uselessly to keep the aerial piranhas away from our faces, cursing, thinking black thoughts, wondering whom we could blame for this hellish persecution. God, was this really a foretaste of what we had come to? With a final wrench we hauled the mattress free, and rushed it up to the bedroom, closing all the windows. Under cover – sleep, sleep. The rest can wait.

Pioneers, o pioneers!

The midges were undoubtedly the most unwelcoming natives of this new world. Strangely no-one had mentioned these ubiquitous inhabitants to us before we set out. But our arrival on that mid-August evening was a swift and fearsome introduction.

The size of this tiny insect is vastly disproportionate to its effect on the animals and humans who share its habitat. *Culicoides impunctatus Goetghbuer* is among the smallest of midge species with a wingspan of barely 14mm. But somehow it does not help to know this nor that each midge only needs one 3-4 minute sip of your blood to feed her eggs and then will leave you in peace. For while bearable perhaps for one or two visitants, the true horror of midges is their numerical presence. On the 4 million or so hectares of blanket bog in the North West Highlands, an estimated 24 million larvae per hectare hunker down for ten months before emerging from a pupa stage for a brief life-span of 20 – 30 days. When one is caught in the midst of a cloud of midges, it is no comfort to reflect that only one species of thirty four in Scotland favours human blood, and only the female at that. To be engulfed by thousands of swarming midges is terrifying because it can induce a level of frenzy verging on madness. The air becomes midge: they are in your eyes, up your nose, in your ears, your mouth, your hair – you cannot sweep your skin clear before another posse lands. The panic is this inescapable, inextinguishable presence – more so even than the biting. Nor is it reassuring to learn that the itching is an effect of one's own body's immune response as it moves to de-toxify the puncture. But the fact is the midge is a native one has to come to terms with. In spite of one or two schemes to eradicate it, none has proved effective. As midges can drift on wind, to clear one area of acidic bogland will not prevent it being re-colonised by a drifting swarm. And whilst big estates in the north-west depend on stalking for economic existence, the terrain is going to remain midge-friendly.

    After our midge welcome, we learnt the necessary armoury and tactics to get us through midge-time. A stockpile of citronella candles was obtained and distributed round the house; fine net curtains were fitted over all windows which opened; insect coils smoked quietly at strategic entry and exit points. As midges come to life as light fades below a certain level, windows and doors were closed at sunset. Outdoor jobs would be re-scheduled to avoid cloudy, moist and warm days. The garden did require daily attention and that meant covering every inch of flesh and improvising a wide-brimmed hat draped with chiffon veil to cover the face. In August this made gardening an unpleasant activity – over-hot, stuffy within the veil, trying to see through the grey cloud around one. I prayed for strong breezes and full sunshine. We did usually manage to avoid the worst, though there was one memorable occasion when we experienced the full frenzied panic. The hay load had come on a lorry too big to get down the final braes. So it was off-loaded by the roadside, and left in scattered heaps where the bales had been hurriedly tossed. We only heard of its arrival once the lorry had gone and as luck would have it, a storm was brewing. It was muggy, heavy, the sky dark with rain cloud. We could only get so many bales in the landrover and we realised that we hadn't time to make the requisite number of trips to get it all down the braes and into the byre. Some thirty yards from where the load had been dropped there was a ruined cottage with part of the roof still intact. We decided to get the hay in there under cover. I can't remember how long it took us to heave endless bales across clumpy ground as the storm threatened. What I do remember all too vividly was the assault of the midges. Working as fast as we could, no scarves, veils or clothes stayed in place – we were easy targets. The conditions were midge-perfect and they attacked in full force. We were choking on midges, breathing them up our noses, deafened by them filling our ears, crazed as they crawled in our hair, up inside our clothing, into every sweaty crease of skin [midges just love sweaty smells!] and everywhere they went they were biting. We were hysterical, screaming, crying, stamping, flinging ourselves in spasms: they were inescapable as long as we were there, and we could not leave and lose a whole load of hay to the rain. It was one of the worst experiences of our time there – these natives we had no wish to get to know; these natives are a veritable plague whose only possible redeeming feature is that their presence has contributed to keeping the Highlands a wilderness area.

Like us, many tourists appear also to be unaware of the ravages of this insect. We were far from the popular tourist centres, but it was campers who ventured down our way. And camping by a sunny river can seem idyllic until dusk. More than once our household budget was enhanced by desperate campers pleading for B&B. Unlike us, the locals displayed far more tolerance towards the midges. Apparently long exposure to midge bites can slow the body's response mechanism and so reduce the itching. I never ceased to be amazed at our neighbours' return from fishing trips liberally freckled in pink spots, but seemingly unperturbed.

But Now Let Me Take You On A Tour Of 'Home'.

To the left, immediately as you entered through that narrow orange double door, was the kitchen moored to its chipped cream Rayburn stove: this was where a guest would sit in the splayed sunken armchair, sipping whiskey: this was where we nursed along the goatling rejected by its mother, scrabbling after it with an empty yoghurt tub to anticipate its peeing: this was where Tim mainly perched, his backside hitched on the stove rail: this was where I dusted the tabletop with flour at the start of the baking regimen – hearth and heart from which the rest of the house emanated into its damper, chillier regions.

Turn right through the front door and you entered a small dank room at first used for storing unopened cardboard boxes, which promptly set to rotting and spilling their contents in ungainly heaps. Later we tried to use it as a dining room, laying a rug over a polythene membrane. By the time we came to leave, the rug had to be clawed up by the handful. Beyond this room lay the large sitting room built by the previous tenants with its roughcut stone fireplace. The room was square and spacious, with a panoramic view through the picture window. But it was also stony cold. The installation of a woodburning stove made the room habitable, but even then its use was mainly limited to infrequent entertaining.

And beyond the sitting room, still heading east, one reached the stable. This contained all the tackle for the ponies, the stalls where they could be fed and harnessed; and eventually the public telephone. After leaving the stable, the telephone line ran for some miles over rock and tussock until it reached a junction box where its signal was translated into radio waves; Ariadne's magic thread back to the outside world. And beyond the stable wall the roof continued over the open-ended woodstore. It was here, some time later, that Tim fired both barrels into a faded old badger who had burrowed under the sawdust and wood shavings after killing our new and inquisitive kitten.

The run of the first floor rooms matched those below. Above the kitchen lay the second best bedroom, which became the first best bedroom at the first sniff of winter, and into which space we contracted our sleeping in order to float on the rising warmth. Over the central rot room was a windowless pod, for dressing in or scurrying through, and then the master bedroom, which had been added at the same time as the sitting room and with the same visionary view, only here with a double bed strategically positioned, it gave a view over the lodge garden, across the inner loch to the angled hills. It was in this summer bedroom that we would lie, gazing into the green-blue-grey world beyond the frame, imagining this as the perfect bed for dying in. From here we could make final, calm, unhurried dispensations – for those at hand, a few last memorable words of consolation and [rehearsed] extempore wit – as our eyes, slowly, peacefully, deliberately irised out on that scene of sustaining grandeur…

By contrast, on nights when the winds roared we lay in bed pondering whether the vaulting eucalyptus trees which rose like sentinels on the hillside behind the cottage would, in falling, be propped and held by the roof's ridge beam or would slice the cottage in half with a single karate chop. Presumably it was all a matter of calculating the angle of incidence… which was beyond us. Instead, in the face of such fearsome turbulence, we could only lie there and idly fret and sweat.

The wettest room in the house was undoubtedly the stone-flagged scullery, which led off the back of the kitchen. This lean-to effort was so damp it could have been tidal. A scrub and whitewash of the walls was overcome within hours by creeping black spores; it

A Tour of 'Home'.

later received a coating of battleship grey fungicide, which baffled nature a little longer. The scullery's rear door led immediately into the hillside. One walked along the back of the cottage over a spongy mulch of dead leaves and brown bottles, tossed there by generations of trees and tenants. Off the scullery was a pokey larder, and in the larder the deepfreeze. This vital piece of equipment was a discarded Walls ice cream container, such as one used to find in little village stores. The reason for having such a modest, venerable freezebox can be put down to the cottage's power supply. The cottage had no mains supply of anything. Electricity was generated by a one and three-quarter kilowatt Lister diesel, housed in a shed by the garden wall. When its starter charge failed, the engine had to be cranked by hand. It gave lighting and one power point. Drainage was to a septic tank located down among – and probably corrupted by – the ponticum roots. Water supply ran directly off the hill to a dammed collection pool, two hundred yards above the cottage.

From the diary:

Yesterday bought a new cassette/radio in Inverness. Was assured of its working on VHF even in our glen. Hah ! Not a bleep on VHF and can get radio 3 only upstairs. So have to have it on the landing with doors open. Reception during the day is awful. And this evening may have been good because the generator is on the blink – so we've spent the evening in candle-blurr-and-fume. Lina at length brought a gas lamp a 9.30. Its fluorescent flat white is almost worse. Terrible day weather-wise. Torrential rain non-stop and winds. Scullery and byre awash.

Domestic Science

This then was the layout of HOME within which we were to live out our Thoreau-inspired dream. For me part of this dream was to discover the age-old rituals of household economy – the grandmotherly skills of baking, bottling, and laundry. The irony of a twentieth century emancipated woman seeking to return to the 'feminine' domestic chores of ages did not escape me; but this was by choice, this was a re-valuation of those skills perhaps too eagerly rejected by more political sisters – or so I reasoned. There was certainly no surviving there without some attempt to establish a self-sufficiency of daily food supplies.

The first stage was to conquer the seemingly unpredictable behaviour of the Rayburn stove as this was the only source of heat, cooking and hot water. The first two weeks were a harsh introduction – the stove would refuse to light, or when lit it would fill the kitchen with acrid smoke; at the key moment of baking, it would go out regardless of fuel. I was distraught as time after time I battled with its idiosyncracies, tears of rage and frustration mingling with those of woodsmoke. My helplessness and the knowledge that without a functioning stove life here was doomed made me even more frantic. Even later on the stove would seize up, often when one or other basic service was also mal-functioning, or when the generator was having its annual service which could take two days, meaning a night with no electricity.

> *Disastrous evening – oil lamps from lodge give nowhere near brightness of light that M's do. Then Rayburn belched smoke from every crevice including the oven until we had to evacuate*

upstairs. Cleaning chimney made no odds and only after a couple of choking hours did T mange to dislodge something somewhere and presto! the oven was at 400 and no trace of smoke in half an hour.

A main problem especially initially with the Rayburn was damp, unseasoned wood. Unfortunately, we inherited an empty woodshed so the first priority was getting in a supply of wood, but that which was most swiftly available for immediate cutting and transporting was rhododendron and pine, neither being good fuel when fresh-cut. After a week of smoke and tears, we embarked on a serious wood search – for fallen or dead, relatively dry, burnable timber. Such a search necessitated day-long expeditions, firstly along the lochside as this would enable a decent quantity of timber to be rolled or tugged down the steep banks to the boat and thus transported to the woodshed. Access to suitable timber and means of getting it out from rock-strewn undergrowth on forty-five degree slopes was to remain a constant exhausting exercise; the need for a daily supply, 365 days a year, meant we were never able to gather sufficient quantity to store a surplus. The anguished whine of the chainsaw was one of the most regular sounds to disturb the rural peace.

    Once I had come to some sort of accommodation with the stove, I set about the supply of fresh bread, biscuits and cake and endeavoured to acquaint myself with the secrets of slow-cooked stews. This did become a genuinely satisfying duty; the magic of sticky dough turning to fragrant bread was a delight, the pleasure of producing home-baked biscuits for visitors, of being able, after a tiring stint outdoors, to relish tea and cake – all this was worth the hours it took to produce it on a regular basis. The kitchen became the heart centre of our life. It was the warm, sweet-smelling [sometimes!], comforting gathering place that was 'home'. It was where visitors would slump in the collapsing easy chair, or perch on the wide window ledge, and drams in hand and kettle on stove, we would pass many a convivial hour of gossip. That was when we would learn about the glen and the folk who lived there, about local history and geography and weather and flora and fauna and how to garden in this climate and rear stock and cook tough venison and where we made the friends who became so important and dear to us.

Another hazard was the water supply. This came to the house via a lengthy black hose which snaked its way up the hill behind to a small dam which had been formed in the burn. The dam was not covered and although a wire net had been wedged across the hose outlet at the base, during heavy rain debris would be swept down into the pool and gradually collect at the outlet, blocking the supply. It was invariably about 11 o'clock at night, when we had just had a bath that the taps would cough and sputter a few leafy spurts of brown muddy water and we would realise with sinking heart that the dam was blocked and that one of us was going to have to get geared up in waterproofs and struggle up the hill in the dark. There was no delaying as the Rayburn had a back boiler and needed a constant flow of water.

The weather would usually be foul, the path muddy and slippery, and the dam overflowing. The hose inlet was some three foot down; by the time one had braced oneself and plunged a bath-warm arm into the icy water, fished around in the tumble of waterfall, hoiked out handfuls of leaf and sticks, plunged again and again, deeper and deeper, one was soaked beyond the shoulder and all down one side. Meantime the wind would be pushing at one and the rain would be doing its best to soak into boots and down one's neck. By the time one had cleared the muck, fought back through lashing branches and slithered back down, all the pleasure of a bath seemed to come at a high price.

The burn did however provide drinking water of a sweetness we learnt to appreciate. As long, that is, as one did not think too much about the possibility of dead deer having fallen in the burn, or other contaminants. It was true that visitors often had upset stomachs for a day or two until their systems adapted to unfiltered pure peaty water, but there was in fact more danger from the antiquated lead piping still installed in parts of the lodge.

So there we were – translated.

14 miles from the nearest settlement or community.
25 miles from the nearest shop, post office, petrol pump.
40 miles from the nearest doctor, garage, vet, railway station.
70 miles from the nearest office of local government, cinema, theatre, bookshop, supermarket, real coffee – ie from what is generally accepted as civilisation.

Yet to be visited, the decaying lodge house, past the cottage, over the burn bridge, up on to the rise where it stood like a plausible holiday home for Norman Bates. Nor have I shown you the walled garden [lying in the opposite direction from the lodge, down past the black shed] which provided the site for my on-going Agon with Nature.

All that is to come, and the people are to come. But until you can summon up the place and its setting in the mind's eye, there is little sense to be made, the images float in a void until one can also envision the landscape in which this new dwelling was embedded.

Landscape

Never before had we sat under such a weight of geography.

The miraculously engineered road, squirming down between lithic boulders, finally swerved to the left to decant us into a version of the promised land. This Shangri-la was a wide, flat, closed and secret place of shallow, pale pasture, grey stone and hunkered homesteads. Ground level, human level, is also sea level. But the mountains seem to burst through the skin of the sea, flexing upwards all around to create a tense musculature. Body builders. We can move as delicately as insects over the face of the water, but to walk on these hills is to sense the iron just beneath your feet. Well before the tops the naked rock appears: black, sweating, adamant. On calm fine days the mountains sink back, reclining into the haze. But when the weather lowers, they lean in and over, grim visaged.

The cottage was pressed like a stud into the base of a hill which rose steeply up behind it for two and a half thousand feet of sog, stones, tufts, ruts, declivities, droppings, rocks, trickles, mosses, heather, lichens, bog, stones like shrapnel, sky eventually. Clambering around and above the house the rhododendron spread its tentacles and out of these rose the mighty eucalyptus trees, with their green grey leaves, as well as pine and birch, whose leaves over the years had fallen and mulched down into a thick brown pulp beneath the tread, and which exuded a damp, fungoid smell which hung permanently in the air around regardless of dry days. The dampness clutched the cottage back and beneath. Plaster flaked off the rear walls, the scullery was streaked with black, carpets rotted on the floor. Books and papers left in unheated rooms crinkled and turned blotchy – as did people. The old Rayburn stove in the kitchen, chipped and crusty, gave a nucleus of heat around which to gather, but the rest of the house, while technically above ground, sustained a cold sweat like a cave.

A burn running off the hillside had been trained to curve round the front of the cottage, running between deep, stone-lined walls. The bouncing water was a constant sound, especially marked at night as we lay in bed – hard to sleep with at first, then strange to be without in other bedrooms. When the burn was in spate after rain, the torrent would carry along stones and small boulders off the hillside, click-clacking together like giant billiard balls.

Opposite the orange front door, clamped on the further bank of the burn, a hefty eucalyptus reared up at an angle of forty five degrees. It seemed amazing that the immense weight of its upper branches had not torn up its roots. Equally surprising that the frequent storms had not managed to topple it; an abandoned swing rope dangled from one of its branches and in the summer it thrummed with invisible bees.

The Lodge

On leaving the cottage door, one crossed ten foot of deer-ravaged 'garden', turned right, and was on the short drive up to the elevated situation of the Lodge, a large unprepossessing and slowly decaying mansion whose days of Edwardian grandeur had long gone.

This public face of the estate was perched on a knoll overlooking the ruins of the landscaped gardens and beyond to the inner loch, itself held behind the pinched rock fingers of the narrows which separated it from the outer loch beyond. The view was a fine one as the timeless features of rock and water do not suffer from human interference and neglect: the immediate surroundings of the lodge have been less fortunate.

The estate had been established by the Captain's great uncle, just after the turn of the twentieth century. He was a wealthy banker with a fancy for the Highlands and a shrewd speculative eye. He sailed his steam yacht up the loch and decided this would be his patch. He was known to the locals as hard but fair. He developed the estate with a fine hunting lodge, new cottages, paths and plantings, and later sold off half the land for the price he had paid for the whole. As he had no children of his own to inherit his interest, the estate passed on to his nephew – at which point began its decline. In its prime the estate had boasted a bevy of resident stalkers, ghillies, gardeners and domestic staff. Walls had been built, ditches dug, paths resurfaced regularly with shingle carried up from the seashore. Exotic trees and shrubs had been imported and carefully tended, complete with printed catalogue [1908]. But the nephew did not share his uncle's passionate commitment to the place, and while taking care to milk it for what income he could [by letting the shooting rights to wealthy acquaintances], he never reinvested any of the capital gained in the upkeep of the estate. And as with other estates, the Great War was a death knell: quite simply, the workers never returned, nor were they replaced. So ditches choked, fences fell, shrubs outgrew their strength, the ponticum spread like cancer. This state of neglect proceeded throughout the thirty odd years of the nephew's tenure. Then the burden passed on to his third son, the Captain – and our laird. He was an enthusiastic deer hunter and professed a real feeling for the place, though this love might properly be termed sentimental as it combined maximum effusiveness with minimum expenditure.

The Captain was, as men say, larger than life. He loomed in the mind's eye. Not only was he broad and heavy in build, his actions were also expansive and peremptory. He was accustomed to use his weight to achieve his purposes, and he expected any obstacles simply to bounce off him. Tales of his physical exploits became family myths.

When everything was running smoothly for him, he was most affable. But at the slightest inconvenience he reacted like a spoilt child, raising his voice and metaphorically [and sometimes actually] stamping his foot. He was particularly impatient with machinery. If a car or boat engine failed to respond instantly, he would throw a tantrum, similarly with an awkward button or a stubborn pony. Like a child he expected the world to revolve around him, people and events to fall in with his demands. If anyone expressed an opinion contrary to what he had in mind, he would pretend not to understand them; the person had become 'difficult'. He was capable of generosity – a little extra money here or there, an expensive purchase for another's comfort [once the idea had become a fixation in his mind] – but in general he was careless of other people's time and feelings, lacking the imagination to see the world from the point of view of those less affluent than himself. He had little foresight or interest in initiating change, for almost any alteration in the political or social status quo would appear to him regrettable. He was naïve and sentimental, and hid these characteristics under a bluff, growling exterior; when he had done something of which he was slightly ashamed, he would give a little shrug and a mischievous schoolboy grin, in expectation of being indulged and forgiven.

He had the misfortune to be afflicted with a degree of deafness, which made him suspicious and irritable in company, where his customary expression was a scowl. He was afraid of missing something or being taken advantage of, but his deafness was also a defence: he just did not 'hear' many unwelcome questions.

Being a powerful man he was obviously aware of declining powers, frustrated that his body could not meet the demands he would still make of it. He liked to remind himself of his past prowess by gathering strong young men around him and directing them, being assured of their respect and awe for what he once was. There was very little malice in his make-up, but on occasion his stubbornness could make him seem malicious – once he had taken a dislike to a person or an idea, on whatever flimsy evidence, he would become immoveable. He had the courage of his own prejudices.

> *The Capt. arrived and with usual steam-roller energy has attacked several trees, dug up goathouse drains, managed to wrench the newly-serviced outboard so that the propeller bushing went, cursed the Seagull's broken holding pin, grumbled about Tony's ponies – but won't say a word to Tony – is infuriatingly vague and contradictory, and shouting to him is quite exhausting. Yet he still has something very likeable about him!*

The Captain had known something of the estate when it was flourishing, and one suspects that this is how he saw it still – through a sepia-tinted haze. For while the worms bored in, furniture cracked and splayed, the roof beams turned slowly to powder, the Captain on his ritual yearly visits would sit in the dreary living room with its stained wainscoting and damp sealed books, being waited on by his ancient housekeeper, who served him his breakfast on a tray with chipped china. He sat at his wobbly desk, a dribble of egg yolk on his chin, writing proprietory letters of commanding brusqueness. He walked his hills armed with stick and glass, and observed 'his' deer and their ways. Forms were thus observed.

The lodge interior was cold and cheerless, the food served was usually execrable, only the stiff whiskeys kept the blood circulating. Another form of nostalgic sentimentality had declared that the lodge was more atmospheric without electricity. Thus the small generator provided the lodge with only one light in the kitchen and one plug for the ancient vacuum cleaner [supplied with about a mile of cable]– romance not quite extending to the convenience of the housekeeper.

This was Lina and as she was our immediate neighbour, we were anxious to befriend her. Soon after our arrival we invited her to dinner. She sat forward in her chair, curled inwards, rather like a mollusc deprived of its protective shell. She never seemed to relax. She had been living on the estate, watching it slowly but inevitably decay around her, for fifty years. She must be so lonely, people would say, living up in that huge cold house all on her own. No, she would say, she really had little time when she was not busy. She sat indeed like a shy schoolgirl of seventy, twisting her coffee cup in her hands. Only those hands were not a schoolgirl's. They were swollen and twisted so as to be unrecognizable as hands, the price of fifty years of cleaning, washing, stoking, carrying, chopping, sweeping, beating, in a house with sixteen bedrooms, no electricity, and an erratic water supply.

Lina was the genie of the place. Fierce, tough, wizened, she seemed impervious to outer climate and inner sentiment. She had the Captain's telescope set up at the kitchen window, focused on the jetty over the loch: she knew everyone's comings and goings; for one who very rarely left the estate, she was always fully up-to-date on the Glen's gossip. Each morning she would issue forth, muffled in woollens and Wellingtons, passing the cottage on her way to feed her brood of scrawny unproductive chickens. A woman of few words, whenever she had something on her mind, she would preface it with a couple of eggs – to ease the way as t'were. Her method of killing chickens: bind their feet together with string, then twist their necks round and round as if trying to wring water out of them. Only when its head had made a couple of complete revolutions did the chicken become aware – too late – that its kindly mistress had something less tender on her mind.

She had come to the estate from a village on the other side of the loch as a teenage girl who had got into trouble. [Her son was now grown up, a respectable citizen with a family of his own. He worked in a city further south and visited his mother each summer.] Lina had been taken on as a skivvy/maid of all work, looking after the cows and chickens, seldom seen, never heard, bullied by the cook. But now she had outlived all the competition and attained the giddy heights of Housekeeper. She inhabited the gloomy, crumbling warren of the lodge like some busy, furtive little animal. She occupied only one or two rooms herself and allowed very few to see inside them. The lodge kitchen was her parlour, but no effort had been made to make it homely. As if afraid the comfort might debilitate her, she lived in Spartan simplicity. Stone-flagged floor, bare wooden table, only a tradesman's calendar on the flaking plaster wall. The black and ancient coke stove was fed Scrooge quantities of fuel, and was supplemented for cooking by a Calor gas oven. Behind, in the scullery, were the old cracked stone sinks with their rotting wooden draining boards.

Tea with Lina; a blue and white check oilcloth on every surface; chenille-draped chaise longue and little round armchair, both with collapsing frames; rugs of tapestry-like patterns, cut and re-joined regardless of squareness.

Having given four fifths of her life to a family unrelated to her by blood or interest, Lina found it impossible, even undesirable, to separate their ways from her own. There was talk of her retirement – after all she had inherited a neat little cottage in a village down the lochside – but she always fought shy of it. Her position as housekeeper to the Captain gave her status and identity. Detached from it she feared to drift into oblivion. To prove her consistent worth and to put out of the Captain's mind the thoughts she would hate to hear voiced, Lina busied herself round the lodge in a whirl of useless activity. She washed the threadbare carpets, beat dust out of the pillows, pushed a mop through the encircling cobwebs, vigorously clettered her dishes. Everyone said how marvellous she was for her age – no-one being sure what it actually was. How tough, how sharp, how loyal. Fewer people noted the pinching of her features under the winter cold, the curving of her spine, the arthritic swelling of her finger joints. Whatever the rewards might have been for such fidelity, the result of it was a cramped, suspicious character, a fierce but circumscribed intelligence, a stubbornness, a constant fear and expectation of reproof. Her life had been perpetual accommodation to other people's whims. ['But she *loves* doing things for us!' purrs one of the Captain's daughters.] So now her life had no centre of its own, no focus without them and theirs. And these people had reached the point where they no longer wanted her. The faults of her frailty and failing eyesight, her refusal to accept any changes in her domain, outweighed her determination to be needed. She really wasn't 'up to the job' anymore. Symptomatic of her value to the Captain's family was that in fifty years they had never registered her name correctly – still calling her Lena, her sister's name. It was a slip that she had never had the nerve or inclination to correct.

So she continued as long as she might to guard other people's worn-out furniture, to give of her best when her best was no longer sufficient, when her devotion was considered, well, really, a little bit... tiresome. The family all chorused that Lina was quite irreplaceable. At the same time they felt that the decent thing for her to do, at this stage, was to go away and quietly die. Which, eventually, after several abortive attempts at forced removal, is more or less what she did.

The Estate

Outside the lodge, the retreat to the past was reflected in the abandoned garden and policies. The former extensive range of shrubs, gathered from around the world in that time of Edwardian plant hunting, often by the owner in his yacht, was reduced to the manic tentacles of overgrown ponticum rhododendron. The policies – a particularly Scottish term for 'the improved grounds surrounding a country house... from Latin *politia* administration...' [Collins English Dictionary, 'improved' having an ironic connotation here.] – these were a wilderness of entangled undergrowth, towering trees, and unkempt paths winding through. The fences, essential for keeping the deer from eating every fleck of greenery, were in disrepair, only the rhodis had become well-enough entrenched to present vegetation unpalatable even to deer on the otherwise barren hillsides.

From the policies, paths led out in two main directions – along the lochside, and 500' up a natural cleft to the central plateau with its encircling hills. The lochside path led past the boat house, a fragile structure housing the estate's two functioning boats and several others of indefinite status. In contrast, tucked in a tight gully, were the remains of the first owner's boat house for his yacht; this still had two sturdy stone walls, finely built. Further on again, a small bay provided the site of the running moorings for the boats, accessed down a precipitous path. Beyond these work-related features the path took on a more scenic role. Designed as a picturesque walk, it contoured the hillside, gaining height gradually, and was furnished with stone benches at strategic points of view. These views presented a near 360 degree sweep as the path traced round the side of the inner loch. One could look back, past the diminishing lodge, towards the bluff bulk of mountain guarding the approach to the loch head; one could look across to the sheer face of rock on the other side, to the low-built farm crouching behind its few bent pines and the jetty of the adjoining estate with its bright yellow 'banana boat' landing craft anchored off-shore; or one could be teased with peekaboo vistas to the main loch extending to the horizon ahead, glimpsed through sudden nicks of hillside. The path curved inland finally before swinging out round the headland at the narrows onto an elevated point. Here was an inspirational view down the main loch as it widened towards the sea far ahead – it was a view to merit a gasp – the sea ever-changing as the clouds affected the light, the hills dropping down in misty folds like a Chinese water-colour, and the islands floating under the wheeling seabirds. Here too was a seat, for this was the end of the path, and a welcome pause. This spot was a favourite with everyone, and indeed on a fine day the panoramic view would be hard to beat. Of course, it was not always fine, and when the westerlies were up and the rain was down, one could only negotiate the point on all fours, hanging on grimly to grass tufts and rocks as one crawled between the sharp drop to the water 200' below and the wet and slippery hillside. For, although it was the end of the path, it was not the end of the route overland to a cottage on the lochside, two bays along. This continuation however was not for Edwardian ladies as it involved a forty minute stumble across rock-strewn and boggy terrain and, if the bridge had collapsed again, a hazardous leapfrogging over boulders and foam to cross the river before reaching the relative safety of the beach. The cottage was one of two still habitable on the estate, the other being several miles further along the lochside and accessible only by boat. Both were in idyllic locations in fine weather, tucked out of the prevailing wind, virtually on the shore, surrounded by natural greensward.

> *Down to the cottage to check and turn off water. Saw seals very close up by creeping along knoll behind their rocks. Pups*

have beautiful fawn-grey-gold coats and are very appealing. Must admit though that the adults when wet look like huge slugs – not so appealing ! Raised a flock of herons and seals saw us. What myopic inquisitiveness and stretching necks, and how they lie there unconcerned curling and uncurling their tails. Amazing to think that they swim so easily with that bulk. Hills turning – bracken golden brown, and dead bog asphodel gold-headed among green grasses. Blue Scabies everywhere, Grass of Parnassus and Golden Rod. Very quiet: inside the cottage just the hum of one's own head; outside the sounds of water and birds flapping on it, a solitary seal splashing gently. Wonderful.

This cottage and the other one way up the loch were now holiday bases for two branches of the family, but had originally housed the gardener and the stalker. One's admiration grew for those stalwart men who could row down the loch, whatever the wind and tide, before embarking on a full day on the hill or in the gardens.

The other path from the policies led steeply up behind the lodge, up and up and up to emerge at last from its cleft onto an extensive plateau where it soon split into two. One path led westwards towards a small hamlet on the lochside some thirteen miles away, but a bare quarter mile along it split again to veer off to the left and descend to the cottage mentioned above, or to wind up to the top of one of the three main mountains contained within the estate boundaries. This mountain ran along the side of the loch, tumbling precipitously down to the water on one side and on the inland side, dropping to a series of terraced rough and boggy dips with occasional outcrops of straggly trees. Near the top of this hill, on a narrow level, was a hidden lochan extending almost to the edges of the available space, forming an infinity pool effect on the loch side, and lapping at the foot of a steep black cliff of rock behind. From this airy height one could see seven lochs as one stared inland – the main loch below, the lochan at one's feet and then in decreasing visibility five glints of water at irregular intervals extending to the horizon. Seawards, one looked to Skye and the Cuillins, jagged on the skyline. Or one could lie on one's front on the narrow space between the lochan's black waters and the cliff edge and scan the fjord below; the blue loch, the islands, the miniature cottage on the pencil line path on the other shore. The wind would produce its own symphony of breathy variations; the gulls and terns below dipped and soared; occasionally a boat would crawl up the loch, and one would realise how insignificant was human presence in this wilderness. On really hot days, the lochan was a tempting pool after the sweat of climbing up to it. But its deep dark waters held a menace which made for quick dips – who knew what spiny monsters might lurk in its depths ready to drag one down, down…

Once past the lochan, the rough ridge of the mountain extended ahead, descending only when the elongated fjord opened some miles further on to a grand sweeping bay and out to the sea itself. The ridge appeared to be more or less level, but the hidden crevices and gullies made for challenging progress. Very occasionally, as dictated by wind and weather, a stalking party would spy deer on the loch face of this hill. An advance spying party would have been out on the loch itself early in the day, scanning the hillside. Stalking on this vertiginous ground was treacherous. There was little cover, the terrain was exhausting and a slip could see you tumbling down a rock-strewn slope towards the loch below. If the party was fortunate enough to get a deer, it had to be dragged down the long bumpy ankle-twisting, knee-jerking hillside where when you looked at your feet, you would appear to be suspended in mid-air over the chuckling water far below. Then there was the problem of the limited number of places where the boat could get in close enough to collect the carcass. Attempts to pull in elsewhere were always a disaster – the boat motor would entangle in weed, the sheer logistics of heaving the weight of a dead deer across the gap from unstable footing in bog or boulder to a moving boat several feet below was often a challenge too far, with the deer or the hunters landing in the water instead. And more often than not, once the beast had been heaved aboard, its weight would ground the boat on the rocks. All in all, this was not a favourite stalking area on the estate.

The other branch of the main path on the plateau led northwards into a corrie guarded by the two other mountains linked by a sharp-edged ridge which formed the curving back of the corrie. This was the wildest part of the estate; the two mountains were formidable, though on the smooth green flank of one a sharply incised zigzag path led to a stalking wall built along a length of high contour. This was the main stalking area and the scene of many triumphs and mishaps. The wall was ingeniously placed to command a view of the favourite haunts of the deer in the corrie. A good shot, early on a good day, in good light and on accessible ground could bring the happy hunters home for tea with time to spare. A bad shot here late in the day could mean a long and fearsome scramble on the ridge in the encroaching darkness to locate and despatch the wounded animal. There was then the problem of dragging the dead weight of a large beast down over tortuous terrain, across bog and rock to the ponies waiting far below. And even then, with light gone, with the inevitable rain and mist setting in, there was the challenge of finding the path in the floundering bog, and the long trek down to the lodge. The second scenario was, alas, the more familiar.

> *An eventful day. Up C'vor to collect a hind Tim had left from yesterday. Just outside the policies we saw a hind with a broken leg which we've seen on the lochside before, so Tim shot it. We carried on up, edged over the brow of the path, carefully approaching carcass in case a fox there, when a huge eagle flew out of the bank not ten yards away. Beautiful gold and tawny-fleck markings – and huge talons. What a thrill*

to see one so close. It had torn at the shot wound on the shoulder and had the bone quite clean.

Across the plateau wound a river course, in dry weather it was a gentle, crystal clear flow, the colours of the stones and the waving fronds of water weeds sharply defined in the shallows. It provided idyllic picnicking spots on the mossy banks, with one spectacular deep pool for skinny dipping, and a panoramic vista of receding mountain ridges as backdrop. But in wet weather the river turned into a raging torrent as it gathered the water pouring down from the surrounding hills. The warm boulders on which one perched with feet dangling in the trickling and gurgling pools, became bulwarks against which the roaring waters crashed into foaming waves and jets. The noise was deafening. At one point the main path west crossed the river; sticking out from the mud and steep banks were the rusted iron stanchions of a former bridge, but now there was only one way to cross – through the water. Although some 20' wide and bouldery, this was not a problem in dry times; but stalking takes place in late summer and autumn into winter and, invariably, it is wet.

On pony duty, I would arrive at the crossing point, ponies in tow, cursing the decision to stalk on that end of the estate, and stare mesmerised at the speeding water and surging froth at my feet. The Garron ponies are sturdy creatures but even they would tug at the rope and turn towards home. I would take a deep breath, a swift prayer, stick in one hand, two ponies' ropes in the other, and into the force of the current I stepped. It was at such times that I was made terrifyingly aware of the power of water as a natural force; one bad slip and one would be swept helplessly along and smashed against rock and fallen trees. It was a challenge; steeling nerve over panic, I would secure one foothold, lean against the flow and try for firm anchorage before letting go the bank with the other foot. Sliding this one alongside the first, the stick pushed hard down, I would try to steady my weight before pulling the first foot back from the current's force to feel about for the next solid, non-slip surface; the ponies, finding their own way, would plunge past in a shower of water and flying rope – letting them go, I would wobble perilously, struggling to maintain balance, and continue the slow, hesitant progress, foot stick foot, to mid-stream; no panic now, just fierce concentration on the tense minute adjustments of weight, angle of lean, balance – out of time, out of self – just dogged focus on countering the sideways force to keep upright and grope forwards. And still the rain fell and the wind blew and of course the water got into one's boots. And then… the realisation that one was going to have to do this again in reverse an hour or so later with deer-laden ponies. Or even later and in the dark.

Yet it has to be said that each of the available stalking areas could present challenging days on the hill. This of course was, for some, what it was all about. It provided good dinner table tales of derring-do. But we would listen enviously to the accounts of stalks on the neighbouring estate conducted with efficiency and professionalism, and invariably ending in an adventure-free arrival home for tea in the light.

> Went stalking with Tim – first time, and probably last! Quite exhausting, creeping about in that immensity of space, whispering. We were soaked before we were up C'vor, then it cleared and was magnificent. The hills are bronze with dying bracken, the green fading, but darkly. It was clear and bright, a perfect autumn day. We stalked a stag lost amid hinds across Buidhe Bhein, gave up then went along the knife edge to S'dail. Saw suitable beast with only two or three hinds and climbed down towards it. Just as we left the top, a dense cloud filled the corrie and by the time Tim had got lined up on the stag, the cloud delivered fierce hail and sleet. The sound of it hitting Tim's waterproof alerted the hinds, and they were all off. I was meanwhile huddled

behind a boulder, freezing. The return home down S'dail was nightmarish – grass sodden so my wellies slid everywhere, driving rain made my glasses useless etc. Jean saved the day by meeting us on the path and her cheeriness got us swiftly back. We had a very pleasant evening with her, gossiping about the glen.

INTERLUDE 2

A Guide to Deer and the Stalker's Duties

As far back as men can remember, large and permanent communities of red deer have scraped a living off these scrawny mountainsides. In the summer, pestered by heat and warble flies, they seek the highest tops for any coolness; in winter they are driven down by the blasting winds to forage for shrunken vegetation beneath the snow. Though one might have thought their problems are sufficient, with the climate and poor feeding taking toll of their young and aged, they also have for several months of the year to contend with high velocity rifles, whose telescopic sights are lined up on them from behind convenient rocks, if ever they relax their vigilance.

When a deer is shot it makes no sound. It will run or crumple, according to where it is hit. There is little to see of the wreckage inside. Only afterwards, with the skinning and butchering, is it possible to check with accuracy the path of the bullet – which may have exploded some intestine, paralysed the spinal column, or raked the ribcage, smashing successive bones like a car running through palings. The beasts just seem to absorb the blow and the pain, like sacks. It's deceptive. If they are hit, say, in the front legs, they are more likely to run uphill – and vice versa – in an effort to ease the weight on the torn limb. And even on three good legs they can outrun you or me. If they are critically hit – for instance in the abdomen – they will probably move off for a short distance then settle down to die in peace and private. In this event it is best to wait for several minutes so as not to drive them further away. They can be readily tracked by splashes of blood on the ground. Sometimes most dramatic can be the effect of a shot through the heart, when the beast will leap forward, racing on for several paces, then abruptly collapse. But whatever the reaction, you are most unlikely to hear the animal utter any cry.

The first step in gralloching a deer is to bleed it – that is, to extract as much of the blood as possible to prevent its clotting and spoiling the meat. Make a slit in the throat not far from the breastbone and sever the main artery in the neck. Bleeding is more effective if the head of the beast is on a lower level than the body to allow the blood to flow down and out. Next insert the tip of your knife blade into the belly of the beast, an inch or two below the rib cage, without stabbing too deep but just enough to allow your first two fingers to slide into the gap under the skin. With these two fingers guiding the back of the blade to prevent its puncturing any of the internal organs, ease the knife straight down the centre of the abdomen, opening up a gap of about twenty inches. With this move of course, the stomach and intestines will start pushing their way out. Again taking care not to puncture them, pull out the coiled intestines, the stomach bags, the bladder, the spleen. It is essential not to burst any of these items otherwise their contents, spread about the inside of the carcass, will require meticulous cleaning out. Depending on where the deer has been shot, the abdomen may also be fairly bloody. If so, this blood should also be encouraged to flow out, leaving the whole cavity as clear as possible. The organs within the diaphragm – heart, lungs and liver – are left undisturbed. The kidneys should also be left intact, as well as the penis and testicles on a stag. It was once customary to remove these parts with the rest of the gralloch, but now that a ready market has been found for them, they should be left in place. [It is said that they are used in a decoction sold in the Far East and recognised as a notable aid to male sexual potency.] Sometimes at this stage the lower limbs of the beast, front and back, are severed at the joint and twisted off, to be left on the hill for other deer to gnaw at. But some people prefer to leave this job as part of the larder work. So once the gralloch has been laid clear of the carcass, there only remains to knot a rope through the tendons of the hind legs, ready for dragging the beast down the hillside.

The deer have brown coats of coarse wiry fur, excellent for repelling wind and water. Each follicle however is a hollow stem which becomes brittle when dry. For this reason deerskins do not make very good rugs: these stems break off as they become desiccated, leaving unsightly patches of rubbed hide. Deer tusks, or tushes, the rear incisors of both stags and hinds, are prized for the making of personal jewellery – cuff-links, dress-studs, tie pins etc. These teeth can be most readily extracted from the dead animal's mouth by wedging a small piece of wood against the side of the tooth and giving a smart rap with a hammer or similar tool. Care must be taken not to hit the tooth directly with any metal object likely to scratch the enamel as such damage will seriously impair the value of the tusks on the open market.

Of course the most highly rated trophy from the deerhunt is the head – ie the pair of antlers intact. These can be fashioned into hat racks, ornamental crooks, brooches, buttons, paper knives, pen holders, ashtrays – or simply displayed as monuments to human prowess. Individual antlers are less valuable than complete sets, so that it is important to remove them in one piece. This may sound tricky, but in practice is quite straight forward. First the skin is cut away from the top of the scalp, from over the muzzle, the cranium, around the eyes, and down the back of the skull. [It is also easier if you cut off the ears at this stage.] The skin has to be removed in this way to avoid fur clogging the sawblade. Then it is a relatively simple matter to saw through the skull itself. If you take a line across the middle of one eye socket, aiming for the middle of the other, nudging the eyeball aside, you should achieve a straight and even cut, giving a triangular slice of bone which supports the antlers at

Interlude 2

the top two corners, and provides a flat base suitable for mounting the exhibit on a board. Of course, even after this operation, there will still be unwanted slivers of flesh and gristle on the fluted bone, but these can readily be dealt with by setting the trophy in a pan of boiling water for an hour or two. This will loosen any unwanted matter [best to leave the window open to evacuate the smell], and then a wash in the nearest burn, or an overnight dip in an anthill, will give your head its final pristine appearance.

Settling In

Ponies

Two ponies came with the estate and the job. On the near-vertical slopes and inaccessible tracks of bog, they were the only way of getting the shot deer off the hill and they were thus an essential element in the stalking enterprise. When we arrived there was only one pony, the other having recently expired, so our first task was to acquire a second. Although I had been through the common infatuation with ponies as a young girl, the responsibility of choosing a suitable working beast was daunting. The Highland pony, or Garron, is a breed which has developed in the Highlands to suit the demands of the terrain and work on crofts, forests and stalking. It has a sturdy, stocky build, not often over 14 hands high, and for all its solidity is amazingly sure-footed. In temperament it is patient and docile – usually!

We began our search by asking our experienced neighbours on the adjoining estate, and by trawling the ads in the local papers. Then word-of-mouth information came via the postie – someone had heard from someone that a stables along Loch Ness had a pony to sell. We set off on a fine sunny day, the lochside birches green and glittering, the loch smoothly reflecting the blue of a clear sky – no ripple of a monster! Winding our way round the inlets we arrived at a professional-looking outfit perched high above the loch. Our ignorance and gullibility, however, led to the purchase of a rather dubious creature. Rhumac was a mature mare, and looked in her yellowing grey colouring and drooping head as if the thought of clambering over a 45 degree hillside was not her idea of a good life: she gave us her 'you won't want me' stance, slouching heavily to one side. Indeed, the appearance was persuasive, but so also were two factors – the stalking season was due to start in a few weeks, and she was in foal. We were in a hurry and Rhumac's disadvantages were offset by her reputation as a good stalking pony and the prospect of a foal which could over time be trained up as Rhumac retired. We bought her. And our faith was not entirely mis-placed: Rhumac proved a morose and reluctant worker, but faced with impossible weather and terrain, she was utterly reliable. And her foal was a beauty.

So Rhumac arrived to join Prince, also getting on a bit, and the two seemed to tolerate each other well enough. At least Rhumac's company stopped Prince wandering fifteen miles up the glen to find other equine companions – a tedious habit as it necessitated one of us – me – in taking a day to find him and fetch him back. Our next hurdle in pony-care was to learn how to fit the deer saddles. These bear little resemblance to a riding saddle as they are designed to disperse the weight of a full-grown stag in a way which will not impede the pony's balance and agility. They are heavily padded, with a strap system to fit round the chest and the rump preventing slippage either forward or backwards regardless of uneven and unstable terrain. There are also several straps and loops on the saddle for attaching the deer firmly. We needed a lesson and who better to instruct us than our ghillie neighbour. Carrying some propitiatory cake, we begged Peter to come and help us. It was the first of many calls for help which was unfailingly answered with a mumbled huff and puff, followed by clipped, brisk instructions. It took us several practice sessions whilst we saddled and unsaddled the stoical ponies before we felt we had everything clear; another new procedure which was to become familiar.

The ponies spent most of the year roaming freely over the hills, but in stalking time they worked daily. A few weeks before the first shoot, we would bring them in and ensure they were fit and ready. First, of course, it was catch your pony! As if sensing the approach of hard work, the two wily ponies would disappear, and we would spend long days roaming the 8,000 acres of the estate looking for them. This was pleasant enough on a fine day, in fact it enabled us to discover areas we had not come across before. But more often than not, it was not so pleasant, and we would spot them at the far side of a wide boggy expanse, or heading along a rock-strewn gully, as if to fling us a challenge – 'come and get us – if you can!' While it proved their sure-footedness, we cursed as we sank ankle-deep or stumbled between boulders, and the return was clouded in mutual bad tempers.

Once secured in the stable, we would contact the blacksmith and he would arrive, unload his portable anvil and set to work. We would have a morning soothing and trying to ensure co-operation from the ponies as Bill skilfully held them motionless and attached gleaming new shoes. Rewarded over the following days with extra rations of oats, and exercised daily along the drive, they would be, we hoped, ready for duty. After the stalking had finished in January, we removed the then worn shoes before releasing them to the hill and their freedom.

Did ponies' shoes – what an awful job. Prince's remaining two came off comparatively easily, but Rhumac was another story. She got fed up, kicked out, and I got my hand torn on the clenches – and very painful it is too. It took us a good hour of sheer sweat to get five shoes off the two of them.

On a typical stalking day, the stalking party and Tim would set off as early as they could all be got out of bed and head for whichever area the Captain deemed the best for the day's wind and weather. A time would be agreed on for the ponies to come up later and to which one of the rendez-vous stations. So after lunch, I would saddle up and, kitting myself with sweaters and waterproofs, start up the hill with the two ponies.

At the agreed waiting spot, there would usually be one or two of the earlier group who would have some idea of where the others had started stalking, and hopefully where they now were. A resounding shot or two was always reassuring, but it could be a dreary time of standing about, usually in the rain, not knowing what was happening, waiting for a sign as one endlessly scanned the hills through rain-splashed binoculars. At length there would be a signal to move forward, and our posse would head across rough ground towards the hunters. This was where the ponies came into their own; they would negotiate the broken and unreliable terrain with steady assurance, whilst we humans floundered and cursed alongside. The deer loaded and secured, the ponies would return with no less steadiness, picking their way slowly, balancing their heavy loads as they adjusted to sinking bog or clutches of boulders. The weather never fazed them. And on one momentous occasion Rhumac really showed her quality; the party had been caught by a raging storm whilst retrieving a deer from the lochside. The path, close to the loch, was flooded, waves crashing over it. Rhumac, heavily in foal, a deer on her back, never flinched but seemed to find the track by some sixth sense; the group allowed her to lead and followed in her wake – to safety.

Ponies

Rhumac's foal was born one fine spring morning –

Foal born! Dark grey with black markings on mane and tail. Ugly, huge head and enormous jointed legs. Affectionate and curious, very tottery. Tim found him there when he went to feed the ponies at 9am.

He soon grew into a more co-ordinated and beautiful creature – in fact it was hard to believe unattractive Rhumac had produced such a handsome fellow. But true to her character, she'd done it all quietly, with no problems. We called him Cristo – why I can't recall. He provided us with real pleasure as we watched him develop over the summer, and during the following stalking season he accompanied Rhumac and Prince on their work days, trotting nimbly behind them, getting in the way, biting people's coats and pinching their sandwiches. He was used to being handled and fussed from the start and showed promise of being a worthy successor to Rhumac. Unfortunately, we were not to see his future progress and I still do not know how he fared. But back then he soon allowed me to slip a head collar on and lead him about, though his tameness did lead to one near disastrous event. The trailer was parked at the top of the slightly sloping drive and Tim was leading Cristo past when he remembered something he needed in the house. So he hitched the foal to the trailer bar, telling him to wait a moment. He emerged from the front door to see a panicky Cristo rearing as the trailer lifted when he flung his head up. Before Tim could get to him, Cristo had turned and pulled away and the trailer rolled with him. He bolted down the drive, the trailer swinging and lurching behind him and Tim in desperate pursuit. Alongside the drive were parked four or five cars belonging to visitors at the lodge. Before Tim could catch up, the trailer had bumped and banged against several cars as Cristo swung from one side to another in his frantic efforts to escape. When Tim finally flung himself against the trailer and halted it, Cristo's halter snapped. Yet instead of careering off, the pony stood quivering while Tim slowly approached, and then he buried his head under Tim's arm, nuzzling in and gently whinnying. Tim was dismayed at his own thoughtlessness, and dismayed again when he realised he was going to have to explain the damage to four car owners.

> *A misty grey morning. Cristo, who got out of the field at 6am, is standing sleeping by the leaning tree with the broken swing rope looped over one ear. Head down, body tilted forward, he stands so still. He delights me – his beauty, basic friendliness, and independent character.*

We very rarely rode the ponies ourselves; other than going for a day's trek up the hill to the plateau, the landscape was not conducive to riding, and the time needed to find and catch them also deterred us. During the summer too, the ponies were not shod, so it was only when keen young visitors came to stay that we made the effort.

> *Up S' a Dail looking for ponies for Sarah's ride as it was such a glorious day. Saw them eventually on our return, way up above the path just outside the policies. A very steep climb up the burn and a hair-raising descent. They were with three of Tony's ponies, and while Rhumac and I sedately slithered down this well-nigh vertical slope, the others careered down in a very alarming fashion, crashing into Rhumac and me far too often for safety. But in the end we got a ride to the point and then round to the farm to feed the cats.*

Goats

After that first stalking season, hard upon our arrival, and the departure of the happy hunters, we were able to start thinking about our own projects.

Our vision of self-sufficiency required animals – not the ponies which were the preserve of the estate and the stalking – but more domestic and productive ones. We considered these would be vital to our economy and soothing to the eye as they ruminated placidly in the meadow, reminding us *nouveau paysans* of our closeness to nature and down-to-earth realities.

We thought we would start with goats, which being smaller than cows would be easier to bully. We located an abandoned byre situated along the track on the left of the cottage door, behind the walled garden. It was a neat stone structure with two main stalls below and a hay attic above. The roof was relatively waterproof and a few strategically placed buckets dealt with the main leaks. Below, the years of accumulated muck and rubbish were embedded and tangled – chicken wire, rotting wood, boxes of scallop shells, tins, bottles, and all liberally draped in Dracula-like spiders' webs – it was a choking, coughing, eye-watering job to clear it. A rising puddle of foul-smelling water lay at one end from a blocked drain, and the window frames were falling out or non-existent. Tim cemented in one window frame and concocted another from a corrugated iron window buried in a corner. With sweat and determination, we finally shovelled and swept it into a cleanliness fit for a spare bedroom.

Having prepared suitable housing, we researched the available goat literature thoroughly, memorising all those points of breeding which distinguished a productive animal from a dud. Then we started scanning the local papers again. The first advertisement that caught our eager eyes was from a farmstead more than a hundred miles distant, but as it seemed that any available goats were in short supply, we decided to make the trip. We loaded the Land Rover with straw bales, ropes and cheque book and set out.

It is difficult to remember just when the rain started, but at some point it settled in emphatically, drumming on the canvas roof, blurring and smearing the road ahead: for a hundred miles there, and a hundred miles [in the dark] back.

The farm lay at the end of a stony track curving across treeless fields. We parked at the top of a slope leading down into the yard which looked too mud-succulent ever to get out of. Alongside, the goats were housed in a lean-to shed. There were more than a dozen of different ages, makes and sizes, presided over by a pungent off-white billy. The woman who owned the goats was somewhat over forty and wore an Alice band. Her husband, younger, burly, kept in the background.

'These are the ones for sale,' she said, pointing out a white Saanan and a smaller black and white cross, which kept jumping up on the stall in an effort to avoid the others. The larger white seemed to have a limp.

'Those two are in kid,' the woman said.

We examined the animals with what we hoped looked like a cool and appraising eye – keeping our distance from the suspicious billy. Mentally we compared the features we had memorised with the actual beasts before us. A good milking goat should have wide-set back legs – which these had not; deep hanging udder – which these had not; long soft muzzles and a gentle eye – which these definitely had not; and preferably no horns – which these most certainly had.

'How much are you asking for them?'

'Fifty for the Saanan and forty for the cross. They are in kid.'

'Do you mind if we just discuss it together?'

'Go ahead.'

We agreed that the goats were not perfect – but then where were we going to find better? And both were in kid – was there any guarantee of that? We really did want to start our animal collection as soon as possible. Even if the animals did not quite match up to specification for high milk yielders, perhaps they would give enough? And they were in kid. And we had driven all those miles. And the thought of doing so all over again to some other sodden croft or other. But what about the limp?

'Oh, she just caught her foot on a stone – it'll soon be back to normal. In fact it's almost better already.'

'Ah, I see.'

All those miles... could we really go back empty-handed...?

Without even haggling over the price, we concluded the deal. The woman took us into her kitchen to write out the cheque. The room was small and grubby and presided over by a scruffy green parrot whose droppings had spread beneath its perch, onto the table, onto the chairs, onto most of the surrounding floor space. The bird watched sardonically as we signed away ninety precious pounds, but did not say a word.

It looked as if there might be a problem coaxing the goats into the Land Rover, but the husband, having sighted money, was allowing no hesitation. He swept the goats up in his arms one after the other and bundled them into the Land Rover, whose sides had been padded with the straw bales, and tethered them to one of the roof struts.

Having rid themselves of their unwanted livestock, the farm couple also unloaded a guest they'd had staying. Said he just needed a lift back to the town we would be passing through. On the return journey, squeezed onto the front seat, this unwelcome passenger kept up a patter of inconsequential chat to match the rain on the roof. In the back the goats fretted and butted, became perpetually entangled in each other's ropes, while the enclosed space became filled with the fumes of their piss and pellets.

The goats were our first major mistake: unfortunately, they were not the last. As contributors to the croft economy, they were a disaster from day one.

They soon returned the pristine byre to rustic muck and mess, mainly by fighting with each other. Barriers had to be erected to establish peace, and here in due time, the goats gave birth to their kids. Before then, however, the full realisation of the goats' deficiencies was revealed. Sarah, the large white Saanan, was lame and had dermatitis. We had a frantic month of phone calls to the vet, loaded syringes of anti-biotics sent via the post van, not to forget the wrestling matches between Sarah and both of us whilst we trimmed her appalling hooves. When it came to kidding, she refused to have anything to do with her two kids, kicking them out of the stall, and butting us when we attempted to intervene. The weaker kid promptly died. The other was swiftly transferred to the kitchen and bottle fed from milk grudgingly given by its mother. It was apparent that Sarah was an elderly creature and mothering was no longer her choice. The other goat, Misty, produced two billies.

> *What a day! Gave Duff [dog] a bath and Misty produced two kids! Went to feed at 2pm, gathered some dock leaves from the garden, went into byre to usual bleats from Misty and Sarah – then two tiny high-pitched ones! Very recent, still wet and staggering, but so big. Great excitement – rushed off to tell the Monty's only to learn they'd lost their new foal this morning. Awful weather in the night partly responsible, Tony thinks. However, despite all their efforts, and Bill Wilson's [the blacksmith], the creature died. They are very sad. The weather depresses Tony enough – he looked suicidal.*

The billies presented a dilemma to which we had given little thought. The theory of cottage economy regarding the goats was that they would supply milk and be the start of our herd. Billies were of no use to our herd plans – we did not wish to feed a hefty billy [let alone two] when we could get the goats sired other ways. The two billy kids drank every drop of Misty's milk, and it was soon obvious that she too was far from young. So we had two ageing goats who were not going to be able to produce more kids later and thus get a herd established; we had two hungry billies meaning no milk for us; we had one goat giving reduced milk most of which was needed for the nanny kid – now our only future hope. If we were to have milk and butter and cheese, the billies had to go. They were despatched while the realities of economy were fixed in the mind, and before any softer sentiments could surface. In the cover of dusk we carried their carcasses in a sack to a point overlooking the loch and sent them to a watery grave. We were overcome with remorse on the way back and felt like guilty felons skulking through the shadows. It was not an auspicious start.

For a while we salvaged some sense of productivity. Tinker, the kid in the kitchen, flourished in her cardboard box home next to the Rayburn. She was in danger of becoming another pet rather than nameless stock as she and the dog played peek-a-boo round the furniture. As we spent a good deal of time on our hands and knees following her with a yoghurt tub, or any available receptacle, the dog understandably thought our joining in the games was great fun and the consequent chasing and shouting produced scenes of mayhem. Anyone happening to pass by and glance in our window would have been concerned to see two screaming adults crawling round the floor whilst a large woolly dog – and surely that wasn't a GOAT! – leapt about barking and bleating.

Misty produced enough milk for a good while to enable us to enjoy fresh dairy produce. With an ancient milk separator, cream was skimmed off and collected over a day or two until we had enough to pour it into the glass jar with its wooden paddle suspended from the lid, and turn away until it magically transformed into butter. The cheese making experiments were less successful. Crowdie, the fresh curd cheese, was not a problem, but more ambitious attempts to try for brie [as per our self-sufficiency bible] only resulted in a revolting mass of crawling maggots. We stuck to crowdie. This happy state of productivity was severely curtailed when Misty developed mastitis in one udder. Her milk flow was reduced, we spent a small fortune taking her to the vet, and hours of grisly cleaning of putrid puss oozing from the infected udder. Despite all our ministrations, the udder split and although the condition was eventually cured, the udder remained damaged beyond use.

Misty's udder swelling again so attempt to get vet. Planned to drive to K – phone here out of order – when spotted M on other side. Beetled over to find phone now working. Vet abruptly diagnosed mastitis from my descriptions of symptoms, and appointment for tomorrow – Sunday! I am somewhat panicky now. Tried and tried to milk her but in vain.

Drive to Ft William to vet in ghastly storm after dashing around our morning duties and getting soaked. Stocked up with sprays, dips and even vaccine jab, which T administered to Sarah on return.

We now had two dud goats, a milk supply that did not produce enough for butter or crowdie, and a goatling who would need support – ie feed – for a long time to come before she could contribute anything. We were learning the hard way. The time had come for some serious re-thinking. We had struggled along, convinced with our books and ideas that we could 'do it' on our own. We were beginning to acknowledge our woeful ignorance and value the advice of our new neighbours. And to realise that we were becoming part of a community.

In spite of the fact that we were living in what might be considered one of the remotest spots in the country, it was not by any means a solitary existence. In fact our lives were enriched by a sociability un-imagined in our former urban existence. There, visitors came by invitation or prior arrangement, once or twice a week: here, visitors began to drop in daily. The adjoining estate ran along the opposite loch-side and a jetty served a small flotilla of boats used regularly by its stalkers. If they were down, they would detour round and call in for a cuppa and a chat. Other folk from up the glen, down to fish or for a spin, would also call by. This way they got to know us and we got to know them and all about life in the scattered homesteads and hamlets dotted up the twenty five miles to the main road. It did not initially seem that we were being checked-out, but in such a small community approval and acceptance are crucial to a bearable existence. Without it, one is dangerously isolated; with it one is befriended and supported. It was our good fortune to be accepted and welcomed into the glen. And as time went by, and the seasons and the trials of our new life tested our stamina, the support of our neighbours, both practically and socially, did enable us to survive.

Roddie and Peter

The nearest neighbours when we arrived were Roddie and Peter, two elderly brothers, who lived in the farm across the river. Whilst belonging to the estate, the farm had in effect been their family home for several generations. They had spent their boyhood here, but the farm had been handed to their elder brother and they had become ghillies and estate workers at the main estate house further up the glen. Apart from Roddie's wartime experience as a POW in Italy, they had passed their whole lives among these hills and in retirement they had returned to the farm, now only used as an occasional grazing ground for cattle. The farmhouse was a long low building, its gable end to the loch and the western gales. It opened onto a square cobbled yard with store rooms and an original dairy around it, and on one side a set of stone steps up to a hay loft, which had also once upon a time been used as a school room. For in earlier days there had been a small community here at the head of the loch: two or three cottages next to the farm, and of course the full quota of employees at 'our' estate over the river. When the fishing industry flourished, the loch would be filled with herring boats – enough, it was said, for one to walk across the loch from boat to boat. The school room was testimony to a former era of a busy, populous and thriving little township; a far cry from the present reality of absentee landlords, seasonal stalkers, holiday lets and abandoned wilderness.

Roddie and Peter were old enough to remember the last days of that earlier life and could tell many a tale over a dram on a rainy day. Peter in particular was a walking cyclopedia of local history, genealogical connections, and surrounding geography. Highly intelligent, with a remarkable memory, he was a tall, thin, wiry man, nervy and excitable when on a topic of interest or outrage, but shy in company – or possibly just not prepared to act sociably if he didn't rate the company! He had a personal dignity and pride which refused to grovel to any laird, but at the same time his knowledge of their family histories suggested a contradictory fascination with their world. He was also a fine fiddle player, though by the time we knew him, he rarely performed. It took a lengthy process of request and refusal, enacted ritually at neighbourly gatherings, to persuade him to play. Patiently, folk would beg and cajole, Peter would turn red and curl up on himself, refuse; others would softly whisper, some would call out encouragingly, flattery from all sides as the room quietened and Peter wavered. On the rare occasions when he gave in, a general sigh of pleasure and deep hush matched the haunting melody of a gaelic lament as it filled the room. Those melancholy strains entranced and moved everyone with their ancient echoes of a culture formed largely by sadness and loss, by the rhythms of the sea, with the sounds of the winds and the birds, with its yearning and yet also its rootedness in rock, in endurance. In younger days, Peter had played livelier tunes for the dance, but in his old age it was those traditional songs he returned to, and often the older members of his audience would join him by softly singing their part. It was a true demonstration of the power of music to create and deepen a shared sense of human experience.

In contrast to Peter, Roddie had no obvious artistic or intellectual skills. Where Peter was sharp and angular, Roddie was ruckled and rounded: where Peter was quick and critical, Roddie was relaxed and jovial. If Peter was a knobbly stick, Roddie was a heather bush. But as with heather, there was no softness underneath; Roddie was slowed by arthritis when we met him, somewhat bowed, happy to sit in the smart comfortable chair given to him on his 70th birthday, but still active enough to do his garden and chase the odd escaped bullock. He was more overtly sociable than Peter and as a gardener, he was actively interested in what I was up to over the river in the

Roddie and Peter

old estate walled garden. Both he and Peter found us, as their new neighbours, a source of amused interest. The arrival of the goats [why not a cow?]; the attack on the garden docks; the saddlery of the stalking ponies; the adherence to books for know-how on everything from cabbages to pigs – knowledge which was in their genes – each week provided a new source of entertainment to be viewed through the telescope from their kitchen window, and then discussed at length in our kitchen over a few drams and tea. As we became anxious to learn all we could from the locals, we listened attentively and benefited enormously from the offered advice and assistance. Yet there was a delicacy in the degree of involvement from Roddie and Peter. With their inherent politeness, they never weighed in judgementally, but like true friends they were there when needed.

Cow

And so to our increasing laments at our goat-keeping failure, a process they had watched with a wry pessimism, they wondered – again – why we didn't get a cow. To them, goats were a waste of effort, if we wanted a reliable supply of milk, we needed a cow. A cow seemed more of a challenge to us than goats – it was bigger and more expensive. It took long discussions with Roddie and Peter and, it seemed, with everyone else in the glen, before we were encouraged enough to take up the offer of local knowledge and assistance and acquire a cow. We tossed the self-sufficiency bible on the shelf and put ourselves in the hands of our experienced friends. A key figure in this enterprise was George, the head stalker on the adjoining estate. George and his Irish wife, Marie, lived further up the glen in a small settlement of six houses and a former school house, this latter being the reason why Marie had come to the glen many years before as the school teacher – and whose bubbly Irish joie de vivre had won over bachelor George! Their house was a centre of open-door hospitality and they became dear friends for us. Marie's infectious laugh and cheery welcome complemented George's quiet smile, and while Marie loaded a table with food, George would reach for the dram bottle and stoke up a roaring fire. Whenever we returned from a shopping expedition, we would stop and be comforted by the warmth of their welcome. I don't think we had ever encountered such genuine good nature and profound love of others. It is difficult for me to convey how much they gave to our lives; George, tall and spare in his estate tweeds, always smart, fiercely serious and efficient in his work, but genial and smiling to his guests; Marie with her curly white hair and red cheeks, always ready to laugh, her voice lively, open to life, affectionate but not sentimental – how we valued their friendship and the support they gave us when we needed it.

And the cow purchase was such a moment. With Roddie and Peter, George offered to take us to the market at Fort William, see if there was a suitable candidate, check it over, bid for us, and transport it back in their trailer. We were overcome by such an offer. Our exploits with the goats had given them all hours of amusement, but now they took us seriously in hand.

On the day of the market we were like excited children. We clambered into our aged Land Rover, picked up Roddie and Peter and drove up to meet George and transfer to his new one. As well we arrived at the market with them for this was a confusing new world. We pushed and shoved through the crowds of tough-looking farmers, desperate to keep the familiar caps of our friends in sight. Fortunately, their progress was halted again and again as they met acquaintances and stopped to shout greetings and news into each other's ears, for the din of voices, animal roaring, bleating, baaing, squealing, and the tannoyed gabble of the auctioneer was deafening. How could we ever move round to survey any stock, let alone make an informed choice? How enter into this fever of activity where we knew nothing of the procedures or modus operandi – our spirits sank: was this a big mistake?

We should not have lost faith in our friends of course. They knew the procedures by second nature and it was not long before we were standing at a stall looking at a red-brown heifer, with short horns and a fringe. The three men consulted together, then turned to us:

'She's in calf for the first time, a month or so to go, so you'll have to wait a bit for milk. She could be tricky as it's a first calf, but she looks promising and you would then have a calf to sell. What do you think?'

We thought what they thought – what else.

When the lot was due, we elbowed through to the ring and stood nervously behind the raised metal barrier. Other stock were still being swept in, moved round and sold at a dizzying speed. The cold metal of the bars merely increased the sweat on our hands. As with all auctions, came the niggling fear that with the speed of the action and the incomprehensible sing-song patter of the auctioneer, one would find one had bought the wrong lot – it was a panicky frenzy of emotions. But George knew the game and when 'our' lot was hustled into the sandy circle and stood looking as baffled and nervous as we were, he calmly waited, engaging the auctioneer's eye by some mystical signal until he turned and smiled at us.

'Is she ours?' we asked incredulous. 'Is that it?'

It was. There were smiles and nods all round, and it was with a mixture of delight and relief that we all headed for the café. In the steam and fug, we thanked George and pestered him with questions now our tongues were released from overwhelming nervousness.

And so Henrietta was installed in the byre next to the goats. Yes, we did really call her Henrietta. So much for the resolutions not to treat our 'stock' as pets. But while we projected human qualities onto her in such a way, Henrietta herself never showed any reciprocal feelings of affection. She remained a hill cow and, if anything, resented our attempts to domesticate her. We aimed to use the period before she calved to accustom her to our handling and to establish a regular routine. In the mornings I would set off as usual with bucket and feed, clattering to make my approach obvious and avoid startling her. Into the warmth of the byre, with its smells of hay and manure, the goats rustling and stretching as they got to their feet, Henrietta turning in her stall to eye me suspiciously. I would clamber up the rickety ladder to the loft and fill the hay nets, chattering and singing to create – or so I imagined – a relaxed mood below. Once the goats got their noses stuck into the fresh hay, I would extract what little milk they had to offer and then spend a few minutes stroking and patting Henrietta and handling her small udder. She was quiescent enough, though I suspected more out of passivity than acceptance.

Unless it was really foul weather, we would take her along to the field by the boathouse and let her loose. The field was fenced in a ramshackle way and we had blocked the one or two broken sections. Or so we thought. As a hill cow, Henrietta was accustomed to being with other cows, she was a herd animal with instincts to seek out other stock. We had two memorable occasions when she 'escaped'. The first was at the time of her calving. It may be that on this occasion she was not so much looking for company as seeking out a secluded spot in which to calve. She trampled the fence and chose the dark interior of a rhododendron thicket. This would not have been a problem had we not been instructed by George, Roddie and Peter that if we wanted Henrietta's milk, then we had to remove the calf at birth and bottle feed it or it would take all the available milk. This meant that she had to be in her stall for the birth. On the day, I realised after some frantic searching about the undergrowth, that she was settling in her chosen nook and the moment was nigh. It was all I could do to negotiate the twisting boughs of the rhododendron and scramble in to reach her. I tugged and pleaded –

Henrietta was not moving. She ignored my tears and increasing urgency. I battled my way back through the whipping stems, tripping, scratching my face, banging and floundering out of the morass of tangled stems and boughs. I ran gasping and crying to the Land Rover and drove over to the farm. Roddie and Peter listened, climbed in beside me and back we tore. They smashed their way into the thicket and wasted no time or kindness in pushing and kicking Henrietta to her feet. With sheer physical force they heaved her out of her seclusion and dragged her to the byre. I was distraught, trying to urge gentler treatment, begging them to desist, filled with guilt that I was inflicting this suffering onto the animal. They ignored me, and as Henrietta slumped down onto the hay, they rolled up their sleeves and got ready for the calving. In spite of the stress, she calved fairly easily, only needing a bit of intervention from Roddie, and out slipped a stolid beautifully-formed bull calf. Instantly, Peter scooped it up and transferred it to the adjacent stall. I knew this had to happen, but it grieved me to see Henrietta search for her calf, and I vowed that next time she would keep her calf and to hell with our milk supply.

However, in terms of cottage economy, Roddie and Peter were right and for the next few months we certainly enjoyed a daily fresh supply of milk and, albeit reduced in quantity by sharing it with Bully Beef, the calf, we also had sufficient to make butter and crowdie. It was all very satisfying.

The time came eventually though for us to consider how we were to maintain this supply. Henrietta would need to be in calf again and we therefore had to recognise when she came in season. As there was a suitable bull at the far end of the glen, we had more or less decided in advance that we would prefer to put Henrietta to the bull, rather than call out, at some expense, the AI man. As ever, the theory was fine, we had made contact with the bull's owners, and had arranged to borrow the neighbouring estate's trailer. It all seemed straight forward. What we had not envisaged was that

Henrietta's moment would arrive when Tim was away and I was on my own. What we had also not envisaged was that our ancient Land Rover would not pull the trailer.

At the morning milking, I encountered an unusually frisky Henrietta; having lost half the bucket of milk to one back leg kick, and been swiped in the face with a lashing tail, I drew breath and faced off. Henrietta turned in her stall and eyed me wildly, she tossed her head about, stamped her feet, and swung the tail again. With some apprehension, I studied Henrietta's backside and saw the telltale swelling. I rushed back to the self-sufficiency bible – how long had I got? How long before Tim came home? As I sank into the depths of the creaking armchair, I realised I was going to have to get Henrietta up the glen very soon.

I drove up to George's for advice. Unfortunately, he had to go to Inverness, but I could borrow Land Rover and trailer that day; tomorrow might be tricky as he would need both himself. I had never driven a long-based Land Rover, and had never towed a trailer. George had unproven faith in my abilities and assured me that I could manage. There seemed to be no option: if I wanted Henrietta to get to the bull, I was going to have to take her. With pounding heart I negotiated the vehicles down the narrow braes, praying no-one would come the other way. Once home, I then had to get Henrietta into the trailer, and Henrietta was having none of it. An hour-long battle of strength and wills saw first my tugging a recalcitrant beast to the trailer ramp; then an undignified retreat as Henrietta put her shoulder to the rope and headed back to the byre; I took a dibber of oats and Henrietta danced about trying to get the oats and avoid the ramp; the sudden appearance behind her of the dog – who had ambled out vaguely to see what the commotion was – caused Henrietta to jump forward in fright and suddenly both of us landed in the trailer. The cow tied in, the ramp up, I headed shakily for the kitchen and a strong cup of tea to recover.

Against all expectation, I did manage to get Henrietta up the glen to the bull. Basking in new-found confidence, I returned a few days later to collect Henrietta home – mating mission I trusted achieved. I entered the field and approached Henrietta and the bull, happily grazing together. I had anticipated some difficulty in separating Henrietta from her new companion and had come armed with a bucket of oats. Henrietta was not interested, but the bull sniffed the air and plunged his huge head straight in. I could see the oats disappearing fast before I had a chance of getting hold of Henrietta. Without thinking of the beast I was dealing with, I grabbed the mass of tight curls between the horns and tugged and shouted. I tried to drag the bucket away from underneath, but the bull just nuzzled further in. Only as he finished did he raise his head and snort out a shower of oat dust; only then did I realise just how enormous he was. We stared at each other, the bull snorted again and nudged the bucket roughly, as he heaved towards me – then, as I caught my breath, he turned and ambled back to Henrietta.

But that was not the end of the day's excitements. Having got Henrietta into the trailer with the belated help of the bull's owner, I set off along the winding single-track road. All was well until I came to the final descent down the steep and winding braes. As I edged round a tight bend, the nightmare scenario materialised – I was bumper to bumper with a motorhome grinding its way up. There was nothing for it – one of us was going to have to back to the nearest passing place. If my progress so far had made me feel tentatively less nervous at driving this articulated convoy [and secretly I was even beginning to feel rather proud of my new skill], pride was about to encounter the proverbial fall. The driver of the motorhome, used to the wide lanes of the motorways and caravan club campsites, was in even more of a panic than I was. He gesticulated wildly and helplessly. His wife beside him was screaming hysterically. I looked at the tumbling burn to my right, some thirty feet down in its rocky gorge; to the left was the deep ditch and the rock face. The trailer was half out of sight round the bend behind me. The passing place was fifty yards back. A sense of utter fatalism swept over me: there was no way I could accomplish this feat of manoeuvring without falling into the burn or the ditch, the track was only just wider than the vehicles. The motorhome owner started honking his horn as he revved furiously. I put the Land Rover into reverse and started praying. What had they said about backing trailers at the local show where such an exercise was a key trial for the lads? I inched back, craning to observe the trailer's movement as I slowly moved the wheel one way or the other. I tried to visualise as from outside the nature of the link between Land Rover and trailer, to see it as one integrated whole, its four sets of wheels working together. All sense of fear of myself and of my surroundings were subsumed in sheer concentration as I focused on each movement of the trailer.

And I made it, against all odds! I came back to myself as I made one final adjustment and saw the motorhome roaring and jerking alongside. I found I was trembling violently and laughing. With tears streaming I crept down the remaining braes, honking deliriously at every bend. Fortunately, there were no more dramas and Henrietta was safely returned to her stall. Unfortunately, as it turned out, the main purpose of the expedition bore no fruit – it had to be the AI man after all.

The Garden

The walled garden, designed originally for vegetables and fruit, had long since lost any resemblance to its former order. It was waist high in nettles, brambles and docks, each trying to oust the other by growing as densely and profusely as possible. Protected by the wall from the foraging of deer, the weeds had flourished. There was a faint indication of former pathways, but in effect it was a jungle. One third was wired off for a chicken run, the old housekeeper's domain. The other two thirds were ours for the cultivating. By our third year, one third had been successfully cleared and was producing all the vegetables we could eat. It was a rare success story for us, and took most of my time and energy beyond the house and animals.

['So when am I supposed to be weaving these fabulous rugs??']

Falling asleep by the stove at 9pm! Must be the fresh air – another fine day. I'll never get any weaving done at this rate – just digging. Tim doing drain ditches. Pruned blackcurrants, planted some cuttings – ever hopeful. Spent an age trying to net few remaining cabbages from rabbits. Talking of which, Tim bagged his first rabbit, alas, not from the veg garden.

When we first arrived it was in August, the worst midge-month. I would fix a chiffon scarf over a broad-brimmed hat, cover all flesh with long sleeves, gloves, boots and in the muggy heat, sweltering and sweating, attack the weeds. It was back-breaking digging to start with and a continual fight to keep the weeds from invading each new patch as it was cleared. Although the soil was light and sandy, it was destitute of any nutriment. The manure from the animals was too fresh to use straight on and had to go to the burgeoning compost heap. The only local source of organic matter was seaweed, so at low tide, I would gingerly edge the Land Rover down onto the sandy foreshore and fill it with fork loads of slimy, slithery weed. It impregnated the Land Rover for life. It was another back-breaking task, loading it, unloading it and barrowing it into the garden and onto the meagre patches of fresh soil. But it worked and slowly the patch grew larger and the fertility improved.

> *Seaweeded this morning in snow then sleet – exhausting although it was easier than before as storms have blown great beds of it up to and over the path. Land Rover stuck in the sand and an hour to get it out. Garden now covered in seaweed and needing to be dug in.*
>
> *Tim dug garden. I mucked out goats and started sorting pile of earth/rubble outside garden wall using small chain link mesh as sieve. Not very efficient. Garden path is lethal even with ashes scattered.*

The locals approved of these efforts and supplied seed potatoes, carrot seed, cabbage plants, strawberry plants, all generously given along with copious advice suited to the area. We planted fruit bushes and raspberry canes. The high rainfall and mild temperatures – on the Gulf stream – and the shelter of the walls all contributed to good growth. Slowly, the paths re-appeared and the jungle was pushed back; we began to get a sense of integrated processes – the fast-growing comfrey fed the goats; their manure fed the garden. But we were still not winning the battle against the docks. After months of digging up foot-long roots, carting seaweed for fertiliser, hoofing barrow loads of manure, digging, digging, digging… we [who?] had a revelatory vision – pigs! They would grub up the docks, manure our site, and eventually provide a welcome addition to the freezer. Eureka!

Pigs

However, as with all our eureka moments, it didn't work out quite so neatly. Two stalwart hogs were procured, dog-sized at first and containable within an improvised enclosure. But, alas, that easy route to fertility was not to last; the pigs did not seem interested in digging deep, they grew with astonishing speed, rendering any fencing useless against their weight and determination to reach the more desirable vegetables. The experiment had to be abandoned and the pigs quartered in more substantial housing.

But that was later. First we had to acquire them. We started asking up the glen, 'Where might we get some pigs?' The answer came via someone's cousin who had a croft in Glen Affric. Once again, we loaded up the Land Rover with bales and set off across country. This time it was summer and the route stayed west. It was a glorious ride. The croft too was well-run and the animals there looked in fine fettle. Rory, the owner, led us towards a wooden pen which seemed to be lurching and heaving and generally having trouble staying on the ground. Rory plunged his arms into the squirming, squealing mass of pink piglets which were besieging an enormous sow. Laughing at our bales of straw padding the back of the Land Rover, he scooped up two protesting squealers and dropped them into a sack. 'There's no way a piglet would stay in that vehicle for two minutes,' he grinned as he handed us the sack. 'You're in for a steep learning curve with pigs – but you'll learn fast, you'll have to!'

How right he was.

Tim had made a shelter for them with a wire netted run. The idea was to move it round like a chicken coop, so that the garden could be systematically cleared in neat squares. The piglets thought otherwise and shifted the whole structure as and when they fancied. We would settle them on a grassy patch only to come back an hour later and find they were at the other end of the rough, aiming for the cultivated greens. We soon realised that these were creatures with attitude. A visitor, cooing over their dinky appearance, put out a hand and had her fingers sharply nipped. Strong teeth. Strong everything. And growing stronger. Came the day when we realised that the garden was actually in danger of wipe-out and confronted the necessity of alternative accommodation.

The only secure housing was at the end of the goat byre where a former tenant had kept his sheep dogs. It comprised a solid stone-built stall and a concreted outside run with a chain-link fence. Perfect – once it had been cleared of the usual accumulation of farm debris, another day-long marathon of dust and filth.

This did prove a more lasting set-up than the field shelter and here the piglets grew to hefty pigs over a space of a year or so. However, although the substantial stone structure did contain them, they soon altered it to their advantage. The indoor stall had a good cobbled floor: that came up first. The concrete of the yard took a bit longer, but perseverance seems to be a pig characteristic, and that too was eventually reduced to chunky rubble. Fortunately, the chain-link fence held, though the door was the weak spot. There were memorable occasions when by dint of a good shaking and crashing, the bolt was vibrated out of its holding, and the pigs set out to explore more attractive pastures. This usually happened when we were up the hill and late getting back for their supper. As we staggered down the policy path, we would encounter ghostly pale shapes moving at speed through the trees. At first, this apparition gave us a real fright. Later we came to wonder at which turning exactly would we meet them; the later we were, the higher up the path.

The ponies did not appreciate these meetings and would become agitated and alarmed. The pigs in fact enjoyed alarming ponies. A favourite game was chase the ponies. This was particularly

Pigs

good fun when a large group of Tony's ponies was gathered together. The objective seemed to be to race under and round the ponies, dodging through their legs, as swiftly as possible. They revealed astonishing speed, nimbleness and agility, never getting kicked and leaving the ponies in stampeding uproar. They could keep the pace up for considerable time and only the shaking of the feed dibber would draw them back to captivity.

To curtail these sprightly outings, we changed the bolts on their gate for more secure ones and added a drop latch. This worked well in keeping them contained: unfortunately, it led one time to Tim being contained in the pen with them. The new latch was fixed below a level which could be reached from the inside by reaching over the top. Care had to be taken therefore to ensure a wedge was in position when one entered the pen. The feed was late, the pigs were hungry, Tim took in the pail of water first, the pigs dived for it, he fell against the gate, it crashed to and dislodged the wedge.

With the impact, the latch fell – and Tim was shut in with two very hungry animals. At this stage the pigs were big, around 13 to 14 stone each; they were hungry; the pail had no food in it; they were angry. As I've mentioned, pigs have strong teeth. It was a tricky situation, and Tim's efforts to scale the fence [high], or reach the latch through the wire [no go], or shout for me [out of earshot] while the pigs barged him and grabbed at his trousers making menacing grunts caused Tim considerable anxiety. It was half an hour later when I eventually went to see what was keeping him. Tim was clinging to the top of a corner upright, trying to fend off the pigs with his feet. He had the latch moved that evening.

As the pigs' contribution as gardeners declined to becoming just another source of manure to be cleared out and carted, our focus shifted towards their future as dead meat. We acquired yet another self-help book on charcuterie, and studied the finer arts of curing hams and making black puddings. When their size threatened to overcome the chain-link, and we gauged their weight to be around 20 stone, decisions were taken. We considered whether we could slaughter them ourselves, thus saving them the trauma of being transported to the abattoir some 70 miles away, and saving us the costs and hassle on wintry roads. For it was winter now and the snow was down. We had the means on site and the deer larder to hand. We opted for a quiet, humane and convenient process. We had determined not to be sentimental, having taken care not to engage our affections too far in a relationship that was bound to end in slaughter.

As usual, we consulted our tomes and our neighbours, and gathered a wealth of contradictory advice. If you draw an imaginary line from a pig's left ear across to its right eye, and another from its right ear to its left eye, the lines will cross over the pig's brain, which lies in a modest cavity shaped like a hen's egg. We were assured [by our scribe] that a bullet introduced into this cavity would cause immediate, painless death. Our neighbours preferred the traditional method of piercing the live pig's throat, and allowing it to bleed to death. But we lacked stomach for such authenticity, so I borrowed a .22 rifle and a handful of shells from our neighbour.

The pig pen – or what remained of it – was over a hundred yards from the game larder, which was the obvious place for the butchering. We did not fancy hauling a 20 stone carcass over this distance, and so agreed that the most convenient place to administer the coup would be inside the larder itself. To enlist the cooperation of the pig in this arrangement we only required a dibberful of oats. The plan was simple and benevolent. The pig would be offered this unwonted treat, and whilst his snout was buried in the scrumptious oats, one shot would dispatch him to even happier snuffling grounds. No problem.

And initially there was none – only that the sight of the oats caused both pigs to bustle forward, ready to follow us to the ends of the earth. With some difficulty we extracted our chosen volunteer, and with springy step he trotted after the dibber, along the path and without hesitation into the larder. The dibber was set down and in he dived. While Tim fiddled with the unfamiliar rifle, I stood behind with the sharpest kitchen knife, a metal bowl and a whisk. Even if the pig was to be shot, it had still to be bled immediately afterwards by stabbing the jugular vein. The blood could be collected to make black puddings; the whisk was to stop it clotting when it hit the cold air.

'You'd better hurry,' I said, 'Or the oats will be finished.' In his greedy excitement the pig was indeed gulping down the meal at a great rate. And that was just the trouble. In his eagerness not to miss a crumb, his head moved up, down and roundabout, and although Tim held the rifle's muzzle only a couple of inches from the pig's, the target did not stay in one position for more than a second at a time. It was like the fairground challenge – trying to draw a bead on a pingpong ball bouncing on a waterspray.

With the supply of oats diminishing too rapidly and the pig showing no sign of calming down, Tim realised he would have to be decisive. The next instant that the pig lowered his head to guzzle, Tim lined up the rifle and fired. But the pingpong ball had moved. The pig was shot through the top of his nostril. He screamed with pain and outrage. And he kept on screaming as he blundered about the larder, with spots of blood dripping from his nose. He bumped against things and overturned the remains of his last dinner. Then he headed for the door which for some reason had been left open. Still screaming, still dripping, he lumbered back towards his pen. We two dismayed humans ran after him, carrying bullets, bowl and whisk, trying to head him off, but not sure if in this maddened state he might not be dangerous, still not sure if he might not turn on us, his tormentors. Tim ran cursing, the spent cartridge jamming in the breech as he hastened to reload.

Now that our considered planning had turned into brutal farce, it seemed vital to finish the bloody business as quickly as possible howsoever. The pig came to a momentary halt along the path to the pen beside a filled-in well. Tim swung the rifle round in front of him and fired a second shot, again too low, only smashing more cartilage. More screaming, more horror. God, this was meant to be so simple! But behind the panic there was now more purpose. Tim reloaded swiftly this time. There was nowhere for the poor animal to go. Besides it was probably in shock. Tim raised the rifle a third time, significantly higher and fired. The pig collapsed as if the ground had been cut from under him. Abruptly, conclusively, without another sound.

There was no time to feel relief. It was important to release the blood as soon as possible to prevent the meat from spoiling. Somewhere inside that thick neck lay the main artery. [Was the beast really dead?] Tim took the kitchen knife and sliced into the tough skin. Nothing happened. No gush – only the body of the pig went into convulsions as the nerves twitched into death. [Was it really dead?] Tim hacked and rooted around inside the pig's floppy throat, searching for that elusive jugular, stabbing this way and that in growing frustration. Then at last the knifepoint found its target and the hot blood ran out over his hand.

'Quick – the bowl!'

I bent over to catch the flow. The pig was lying awkwardly on a downhill slope. With its neck on the ground, it was difficult to get the bowl into position. Most of the blood stained and melted the snow. I gamely whisked into bubbles what little we had managed to save. Eventually we both stood up. Body steam mingled with our exerted breath curled into the air. The deed was done. The slaughtered animal, too heavy for the two of us to shift, had come to rest seventy yards away from the larder. We would have to tow it.

Tim manoeuvred the Land Rover back along the path and took a rope from the pig's back legs to the tow bar. While I eased the Land Rover slowly forward, Tim struggled to keep an old fertiliser bag under the body to protect the skin from the stones. Progress was painful. By the time we reached the larder and heaved and humped the carcass into position under the lifting gear, we were both in a sweat. Hauling the pulley rope to raise the body clear of the ground, we found the pig weighed just over nineteen stone.

Tim set to work at once to gut and clean the carcass. He treated it the same as a deer, slicing along the belly to the throat, letting the intestines spill out. Inside, the carcass was strikingly clean. The organs were neat and orderly, contained in their separate membranes. There was hardly any blood. The next task was to scrape this skin. Pigs are covered with stiff, flat bristles which have to be removed before anything can be done with the meat. Again, different methods are advocated – burning straw, boiling water, direct singeing. We thought we would use the almost-boiling-water method, though we were not quite sure how much we would need or how best to apply it. We heated our largest saucepans on the stoked-up Rayburn, then carried them up to the larder. We soaked various rags and cloths and slapped them on the pig's flanks. After waiting a moment for the magic to work, we removed the cloths and set to with a paint scraper. The result was dismal. Odd little tufts of hair would come away, but for the most part we made no impression at all. The skin just started to look blotchy and diseased.

I thought I would be better employed cleaning out the intestines. The scribes had informed us that the membrane enclosing the long intestine was the ideal wrapping for the sausages we were to make from all the tasty off-cuts. I therefore carried this prize, carefully ravelled in our washing bowl, down to the burn where it could most readily be washed out. Tim was glad I had taken it from the larder as its smell and dark grey green colour was beginning to turn his stomach. However, once standing in midstream with the webby skein, metres and metres of it, writhing around me, I discovered a further disadvantage of our timing of this escapade. The burn was so icy cold that first the membrane, then the grey green matter inside, then all my fingers handling the membrane froze into stiffness, and the task became impossible. I decided that perhaps scraping away at a pig's hide with a blunt instrument might, after all, be marginally more rewarding.

'We can always use sausage meat just as sausage meat,' I said, and the remains of the grey green snake was allowed to squirm its way out to sea.

At last, having given up on the almost-boiling method, I headed for the farm and some local advice. With his usual contempt for our books, Roddie dismissed all niceties and told me to pour boiling water over the hide. Of course, by the time it hit the hide, it was off the boil, and the skin shaved clean with no effort.

It was just as we were completing the job and removing the last of the offal from the larder, that we heard the engine overhead. As it came nearer and lower, we went outside to investigate. The helicopter weighed in slowly over the eucalyptus trees. It carried RAF markings and one of the crew sat in the open hatch with his legs dangling over the side of the fuselage. Because of the snowfall, the RAF was evidently checking out the well-being of the remoter inhabitants. The crewman waved. We waved back. Each of us was brandishing a bloody knife and all around us was evidence of carnage, where something like a body had been dragged across the snow. We realised our somewhat compromising situation. But the crewman waved again, as the helicopter banked away.

Shopping

Our chickens produced two tiny eggs!

How self-sufficient is self-sufficient? After a year or so, we had settled into a survival routine and were able to enjoy an erratic provision of milk, butter and a little cheese, vegetables from the garden, eggs, and the occasional fish and venison. For all other staples we had to seek elsewhere: in other words we had to go shopping.

A shopping trip was a serious affair involving a round journey of 140 miles and a day away from base. The logistics were complicated: first extensive lists were accumulated over several weeks, subdivided into essential/if you can find it/if there is time/if there is any money left; then arrangements for milking, feeding animals in our absence – with additional problem of Tinker, the goatling when she was still in the kitchen; finally which vehicle was to be coaxed into making the distance – depending on the nature of goods to be collected and number of passengers.

A typical list might be as follows:

- Collect repaired outboard from marine chandlers
- Spare parts for chain saw/boat motors/generator
- Fencing materials
- Assorted vital tools/nails/bolts
- Replacement buckets/brooms/shovels for lodge
- Feed for goats/cow/pigs/chickens/dog [five month's supply in rotation]
- Pony harness to be dropped off for repair
- Cash & Carry for monthly quantity of
- Flour/cereals/rice/pasta/pulses/sugar etc.

Shopping

Inverness shop with M – my heart sank when she brought the carry cot. We were pretty over-loaded in the end with B's two outboard motors on the roof rack, animal feed and all our two loads of shopping within. I had to leave the petrol hidden among the boxes at the shop for Tim to get on Wed. Consequently it was a slow drive down the glen.

T shopped – found a farm for veg, some good stuff and reasonable, especially carrots for goats at 3p a lb. But no trailer fittings, generator oil or battery, glass etc etc. As Tony says, things take time out here, you just can't expect to do everything in one day's shop, it seems.

INTERLUDE 3

Weather

SOMETHING ABOUT RAIN

It can rain here. Clouds roll in like Michelin men on the south west wind, having sucked up moisture from the flat passing ocean, and this is their first landfall. They try to rise on the warmth from the land, to keep rolling on their way, but the sharp mountains puncture their underbellies, and down it comes, all germens spill at once on the ungrateful heads below. The procession can go on for hours, days, weeks. Rain in rods, rain angled like tracer, rain in a soft soaking veil, endless precipitation, engulfment, tuning the hillsides, raising the waters towards a crescendo that is never reached. A quadraphonic roar – and closer to the ear a delicate percussion of drips from leaves that droop. Insect footfalls. (Tim)

The weather here was not something one took for granted. With a rainfall of 120 inches a year it was a dominating presence, pressing itself into every fibre of our lives, inside as well as out. It ruled what we could do, how we could live. Indoors the damp emanated from the walls, the floor, the misted windows; it permeated every article of clothing, even the rug laid on one floor had to be scraped up in rotting pieces when we left. The stove reacted to adverse winds and rain which stopped the smoke escaping; the back scullery was a dripping cave. Outside there were routines with animals and wood-cutting which had to go ahead regardless of the weather, to say nothing of the stalking. Other activities such as gardening, ditching, patching the decrepit outbuildings, had to be done in between the rains and storms. The entries in my diaries nearly all begin with a note on the weather, but there is not often a longer commentary, its familiarity did not need detailed recording! But here are a few entries which perhaps catch at its immediacy. The crushing depression of sun-less weeks of churning winds and rain [the fjord-like steepness of the hills meant the sun did not reach us until well into the spring] could swing to exhilarated excitement on waking to an unexpected day of brilliant light, shimmering off leaf and loch. Those days were magical, all the more wonderful for the weeks of gloom.

Through the seasons from the diaries:

AUTUMN

A marvellous day – crisp, bright, even saw sun here for a bit. Spent the morning trying to drain the goathouse: cleared shed at back and dug ditches; working so far, but it hasn't rained again yet.

It has rained and blown all week. Everywhere is flooded – paths squelch, one slithers about. Tim took the bull by the horns and dug out ditches on hill path. Wind is still raging, stream roaring past window, and drips all round. We have moved into the study to sleep as mildew was overtaking us in the bedroom. Hens laying well. Duff on heat. Oh my, that wind!

Storm terrific. T left with Lina in Land Rover and virtually sailed down the drive. Water up to garden wall, waves rolling over the drive. Opening and shutting gate, he got his wellies filled and had to come back for dry everything below the waist! Water was washing into cab. Generator house ankle-deep. T had to unblock all drains at 4. One wonders what we will have to do tomorrow in the repairing line.

Interlude 3

Torrential rain and wind continues. Branch fell on the electricity cable from garage to stable and broke holding wire. Scullery flooded. Ponies stampeded Tim in their eagerness to get into the stable.

WINTER

A crisp morning: sky is luminous rose pink above the snowy top of Druim Fada. Quite a lot of snow, Sgurr Dubh opposite is covered for top 2/3rds. In the garden, planted blackcurrant beneath top wall, and finally cleared to the top gateway – satisfying to uncover a path edging going round a corner.

Snow. A magnificent day – sunny and crisp with deep fluffy snow. Walked narrows path. Landscape under snow looks like those old black and white engravings – fine lines, hatching, clearly marked on white.

Walked to the top of braes to meet the post where the snow plough stops. Waited an age; later learnt Postie waiting at fank! No stores therefore. Right mess up. Phone engineer arrived in his working Land Rover to say phone fixed – drove straight across the lawn and sank in.

Even more snow – up to 1ft deep in parts. Generator failed to start at 4.30pm. We plunged through drifts to Ted's boat and stole his Quick Start and a lamp. An Eerie sensation plodding into an unidentifiable waste with a hurricane lamp to guide us back along our footprints. Echoes of Good King Wensleslas!

Thick snow again! Hearts sink however beautiful it may look. Walked to farm to check phone. Off as usual. Tried to get up the braes. Had to grit, sacks under two wheels. Exhausting and very alarming seeing Land Rover sliding slowly downhill sideways-on…

Interlude 3

SPRING

Drove to Inverness to shop. Magnificent day, spring-like in fact, balmy at first, wind chilled later.

Such a gorgeous evening we walked to the narrows after tea. It was idyllic, colours, air, temperature – all perfect, and a wonderful misty sunset. Bridge past boathouse has collapsed due to spate last week.

A lovely spring day. Digging in the morning, then an early lunch and a long walk up the hill. Weather just right for walking – sunny with a light refreshing breeze. Went to the nymph's pool which I'd not found before – quite a place. Waterfall of a good 50' into a big deep green pool.

Glorious day, so warm and balmy. Third in succession! Spring almost perceptible green in the garden, trees, lawn. Lots of gardening been going on. Yesterday evening I walked to the mooring rocks and watched the sunset. Bank by the old boathouse covered in primroses. Foal grows apace – bit me too! Later in the evening we went for a gentle row about the inner loch, tide and wind enabled us to drift much of the time. It was quite perfect.

Hot, muggy, midgy [already!], after night of torrential rain. Tim baled out all boats. Later a walk to the point through green, flowery banks. Bracken stems in unending ranks, ready to unfurl. How marvellous to live here.

SUMMER

Fine weather so have been gardening away. Ted back – had had gales which ripped his mizzen sail to shreds, but he looked pretty happy nonetheless.

A grey day. Drizzly and heavy at first, then very hot. Tonight T's ponies galloping round field because of midges.

Interlude 3

It has rained solidly for a week bar one afternoon when we walked almost to Arnisdale after T's ponies. Got kicked in the backside for my pains, so now have one blue bum. Beautiful day – windy, sunny, bright – and exhausting! Quite different landscape beyond Criach – lush trees, big river, marshy, lochans – lovely.

Sun! Until tea, then the familiar mist rolled along the loch. Getting me down these grey days.

I ache all over after walking to and from Li to collect Duff after his stay with R and H. Yesterday in hot sun to Arnisdale. The riverside below Criannich is a bog now thanks to the Hydro. The hills so green; cows loose on hill; a thundering waterfall and a bridge new-planked. A three hour brisk trek to reach Rick, who in fact came to meet me in his 'new' hand-painted minivan. A long, swelling boat trip with L. curled over the bow. The crossing is further than I'd remembered and very open to wind and current. Had a good warm welcoming evening chatting on mutual interests and dining on Pea Soup [viz Frugal Cookbook]. Felt too dozy in the morning to cross loch early with Rick – it also looked very rough! Left at 10.30 in rain to walk; cleared by 11 then sun and marvellous views. Route across rough lochside was very wet. Once on path it was easier: I love the lone pine trees along the path, the orchids, the sound of the sea on rocks, the wind moving in grass, the grey lichen-patched rocks, the tormentil, the over-flowing burns. A fishing boat trawled up mid-loch.

Interlude 3

TIM'S KINLOCH HOURN DIARY
[For Tony & Miranda 20.01.76]

Monday	We couldn't go stalking for mist on the hills, The postman turned up – with a couple of bills, So we took a wee dram – just a couple of gills, And, oh yes, it was raining again.
Tuesday	Our neighbours' nice ponies pushed open our gate, Which nobody noticed till it was too late' Now what was our garden's not looking so great, And, oh yes, it was raining again.
Wednesday	The woodshed was empty, so – fresh logs to get, And as is quite normal, they're all soaking wet, The kettle's had hours, it's not boiling yet, And, oh yes, it was raining again.
Thursday	The Rayburn got awkward and started to smoke, So we opened the windows, we gave it a poke, We had just two options – to freeze or to choke, And, oh yes, it was raining again.
Friday	The wind in the night blocked the drive with a tree, Which on its way down cut the 'lectricity, While our boat on the mooring got swept out to sea, And, oh yes, it was raining again.
Saturday	The goats have turned fussy and won't eat the hay, The dog chased the chickens, so now they won't lay, While the cats have invited the mice here to stay, And, of course, it was raining again.
Sunday	Today was quite different, I'm not quite sure why, We drove to Moldoun for the Word from on high, And on the way home, not a cloud in the sky, But by tea it was raining again.

Visionaries and Dreamers

Church

Bleak and barren the glen could seem, but this was God's Little Acre nonetheless and He ensured His presence was kept alive and well. Midway down the twisting track to nowhere there was a small hamlet of some eight homes strung alongside the road which formed the boundary between two large estates. Whilst the men on each side maintained a polite working relationship, the families were formidable adversaries of the two dominant faiths of the Highlands – Roman Catholicism and Wee Free Calvinism. In our ecumenical innocence, it took us some time to realise how carefully we had to apportion our visits if we were not to enflame local sensitivities. So whilst we tried to follow a strict alternating pattern to our Sunday calls for tea and gossip, the warm hospitality of the Catholic side with its lively laughter and cosy sitting room soon proved a more engaging attraction than the severe austerity of drawn curtains, yesterday's buns and cold lino in the Wee Free camp. Yet as nominal Anglicans, we were drawn in to the Protestant fold and expected to accompany our upright friends to the only celebration available in the vicinity.

So, every second Sunday in the month, a little before 3.30 in the afternoon, we would join the twenty or thirty people of the glen – together with any interested tourists who might happen to be passing – as they gathered outside the small stone chapel at Moldoun. A bleak little fixture, it stands on a knoll back from the road surrounded by a few pines spared from the buzz saw, and, in the spring, by a few bands of skirmishing daffodils. Across the road, the landscape falls away down to the river in the valley floor and the hills beyond.

In my mind's eye as I write now, the familiar ritual re-plays itself with all the details of setting and sounds as if I were there again. As people get out of their cars, they are assailed by the inevitable wind, which slips inside their jackets, curls beneath their skirts. They greet each other with comments on the weather and enquiries after absent relatives. The men and the women gravitate to separate groups, the men talking of football, the women of families. The arrival of the fresh-faced minister in his yellow VW estate with his wife and small son is the signal for the congregation to move out of the cold into the church, where Euen, acting as warden, directs them to their pews.

The interior of the chapel is unadorned, apart from a bowl of flowers on the window sill. The floor is bare, untreated wood, but the pews are solid, stained and varnished. On the back of one is the ill-erased enquiry written with a steel nib in copperplate – 'I hope you were none the worse of Thursday night Eliza or did you get it from the stranger'. Heating is supplied by a two-bar electric fire. Any item of brass, including the small toggle bracket by which the window sash is secured, is highly polished. Below the pulpit from which the minister conducts the service stands a rather handsome euphonium. Mrs G used to accompany the voices, but now the instrument is defunct. Fortunately the minister is able to lead the singing with his strong, convincing tenor.

When the congregation is settled, the minister makes his brisk entrance down the right aisle, sidestepping the electric fire, to mount to his pulpit. His scrubbed cheeks glowing, his rimless spectacles glinting under the electric bulb which hangs above his lectern, he welcomes everybody to the Lord's House, announces that the recent sale of work/raffle/ teas realised the satisfactory sum of £… [thanks to all concerned] and proposes the psalm with which we shall begin to worship the Lord. With brisk confidence he leads the faltering voices through the verses he has chosen, and those unfamiliar with the tune endeavour to make convincing noises until they can pick it up. The minister's voice rises strongly to the high notes, while several of the congregation hang about on the lower slopes, waiting for him to come back down to a more comfortable level, when they can fade in behind. Usually by the end of the verse, most people are tagging along, though one or two resolutely keep their books closed to avoid any danger of being drawn to give tongue.

At the end of the psalm, the congregation sit with lowered heads as the minister starts into a general prayer supposedly geared to meet the spiritual requirements of this particular collection of souls. The prayer seems to rely on the inspiration of the moment, proceeding with many pauses, sudden little bursts of fluency, and ecclesiastical phrases mixed together with homely reference to local preoccupations; thoughts for the elderly who may be worried by the approaching winter, others named as being in hospital. However long the pauses, the minister does not um and er. His prayer meanders along in a pleasant, undemanding way, with several allusions to our imperfection and unworthiness. One or two of the congregation doze momentarily. Minds wander and then drift back as the prayer winds to its conclusion.

We all sit back, and the minister proceeds to the day's lesson. He reads a little then elucidates, then reads a little further. Bottoms shift to ease on the polished wood. Shiny surface to slip on, and the seat too narrow for leaning back with safety.

At the conclusion of his reading, the minister announces the hymn to be sung. Depending on his confidence to lead us through the oddly dipping tune, we almost falter to a halt when he loses concentration for a moment and repeats the first line of one verse. His wife in the middle of the congregation looks up sharply. But the slip is past, the right line is recovered and the journey through the hymn completed.

Now we can sit back for our longest period of privacy as the minister embarks upon his address. While he speaks, two flies walk up the diagonal of the diamond-shaped leaded window. Then they buzz to the bottom of the frame and start up again. Left to right. The minister's wife puts on her gloves, then takes them off. Hisses to her son to stop whatever he is doing. Her husband's preaching hands move from his pulpit to his glasses, to his trouser pockets, and back to the pulpit, where he gradually pushes his Bible further and further along the handrail to the right. He winds up his address with a sententious little quotation, and adds –

'Very beautiful and telling words, I think.'

Finally –

'Your contributions will now be received.'

He sits down almost out of sight, as the warden moves down the side aisle, thrusting his long-handled collection box along the rows.

When the money is all in, the final hymn is announced. This time a more rousing and familiar tune, which the congregation attacks with renewed energy, the end being now in sight.

Then after a swift blessing, the minister exits past the electric fire. A moment or two is allowed for private prayer, and the warden steps out to unplug the fire till next month. All file out past the smiling minister, who, having shed his authoritative pulpit air, appears as a pleasant young man with bright teeth. He shakes every hand and gives an appropriate word of greeting. The afternoon is now colder and conversations are carried on sideways as people edge towards the shelter of their cars.

'Would you like to come round for a cup of tea?'

Comforting words, which for some [like us?] justify the whole expedition.

The James'

But if the protestant church fostered a communal spirit, there were those who were excluded from this fold, the Roman Catholics. Not that one Catholic family in particular saw it that way. Asked once if they didn't feel themselves cut off from the rest of the glen, the reply came sharp and swift –

'We *are* the glen. No other family has been living here as long as ours has.'

Yet in other respects too, the James family *were* cut off from the majority of the community. As church-going provided a social focus for a large section of the community, a family that joined a Sunday gathering outside of the glen was bound to appear somewhat 'different'. In addition, their family connections and the entrepreneurial nature of their enterprises marked them out from other families – whether crofters, stalkers or ghillies – as folk who were on their own. And for a start to get to their place you had to row across the river! Halfway up the glen, as the road skirts an inland loch, you saw a notice advertising an activity centre with instructions on how to reach it: go down through the forestry plantation to the lochside, take a boat and row across to the other side.

We had had little regular contact with the James', but they were a presence in any talk of the glen and its recent history and we were keen to meet them. Then an opportune invite to supper arose and one balmy summer evening we made our way through the new plantation towards the gently rippling water below. We were shocked to see how the native birch trees had been scored with an axe round the trunk, thus ensuring their demise – and space for more conifers. This was a privately owned plantation – or rather an investment opportunity – a result of a government initiative then accounting for the acres of 'wild' hillside being bulldozed and planted in dense monoculture. Like many other inhabitants, the James' had protested against being enclosed by dark curtains of pine, but to no avail.

On that summer evening we rowed slowly upstream against a gentle current towards the rough landing stage. We then walked for quarter of a mile to the house, passing on the way a small black calf and a tiny goatling grazing side by side under the watchful eye of the calf's mother. The house consisted of a random hotchpotch of accommodation set on rising ground with a stream running past its west front. Flowers, fruit trees, a distant vegetable plot, two ponies leaning over the fence to crop the greener grass, and a tranquil view down the valley; a world seemingly on its own. It had something of the vision *we* had hoped to achieve.

We were ushered into the family sitting room around typical clutter towards a fine peat fire. For a while we talked about peat cutting, where it was done, the art of it, the technical terms, the difference in implements used, the variable quality. As Mike had been working his patch for a few years now, the peats were getting better. They certainly burnt well and scented the room.

We moved into the kitchen for supper, and various other members of the family and guests appeared from different parts of the warren. Two cartwheel-sized quiches, a generous dish of potatoes, corn on the cob which squirted its buttery juices right across the table when bitten into, and cans of beer or fresh milk with floating gobbets of cream to drink. As an unusual dessert, Lucy, one of the working guests, served up elderflower fritters.

'They smell of cat,' said Dee, aged eight, the youngest of the James' children. He bit into one. 'They taste of cat too.' He continued to eat nonetheless.

Deep fried, the sprigs of elderflower came out crisp and crenellated, delicious with sugar and syrup.

'They taste like the smell of a hedgerow in the morning,'

volunteered a young man behind a curtain of dark hair. It sounded more inviting than cat.

'I suppose they have special qualities which are good for us?' asked Bell James.

"fraid so,' smiled Lucy. 'They're good for the eyes, the nerves and the skin – and they're a relaxant and a bit of a soporific too.'

'Nobody will be able to get up in the morning.'

'No – have to explain that the elderflower got us!'

After the meal everyone dispersed once more to their separate quarters and we settled with Mike and Bell back by the fire. Once prompted, Mike began to expatiate on the glen, its former flourishing state and subsequent decline which he attributed mainly to governmental mismanagement. He described what sounded like Eden before the Fall – a terrain abounding in rabbits and small game serving to feed the bigger, wilder game – the kites, the cats, the martens. In pre-war times, when Mike was a child, you couldn't drive along the roads at night [if you happened to be in one of just two cars in the glen at that time] without coming across some wild hunter caught in your headlights.

'You couldn't walk from here to Greenpasture without putting up three or four pairs of grouse, more if you had a dog with you rummaging around – and all those blackcock flying over too. At a conservative estimate, six thousand salmon would pass up the river each year to the higher spawning grounds; the trout in Loch Q were famous for their availability and regular 1-2lb size. And come the winter, the hinds would be down to feed around the loch in great herds…'

So, what had led to the loss of this abundance? First, myxomatosis, which killed off all the rabbits; so the game that had fed on the rabbits turned on the other small animals and mostly wiped them out, and then when there was nothing left to eat, they died out themselves.

Then came the hydro scheme and, in spite of all the assurances,

The James'

the salmon fishing was ruined. And after that the Forestry bought up and enclosed what used to be the deer's winter grazing, changing the pattern of deer movement in the area.

'So from a conservation point of view, the glen has really been ruined...'

All around them the James' see little but loss. Back towards the beginning of the century, a branch of Mike's family had owned the whole glen from the main road down to the sea. But family fortunes were decimated by the Great War [four out of five sons killed] and by the slump of the thirties. By the end of the Second World War, the estate was fragmented into smaller holdings, and responsibility for the management of the remaining property had largely passed into the hands of surviving female members of the family who had comparatively slight interest in developing the sporting or other potential of the land. When Mike came out of the army, around 1960, he took over the lease of this croft, at that time just a ruin. He and Bell – also from a local family – set to rebuilding the croft virtually from the ground up. After making the place habitable for themselves and a growing family, they went on to superimpose on the original croft, with its modest six acres and common grazing, an outdoor [adventure] holiday centre offering riding, sailing, climbing, shooting, stalking, camping, walking, to as many as thirty-five visitors at a time. The croft supplied all the centre's needs for dairy, meat, vegetables, soft fruit, fish. Wasn't this a success story?

There was another factor which, paradoxically, isolated them – a positive drive to foster the spirit of community. Where most people here tacitly assumed a spirit of community and co-operation, Mike articulated it and attempted to build practical schemes upon it. His desire to see a thriving communal identity manifested itself in his knowledge of the glen's history, in his wish to see its traditions preserved, in his encouragement of his children to learn Gaelic and perform readily at glen ceilidhs, in his family's recent participation in ecumenical gatherings, and perhaps most ambitiously in his involvement with the Moldoun Hotel, the one and only hostelry in the glen.

From earlier family ownership, the hotel had fallen into the hands of a succession of speculators whose grandiose money-making plans seldom came to anything. Eventually Mike persuaded a young Frenchman, a financial cruiser, to buy the hotel and then rent it back to him for a two year trial period. Mike's own plans were, however, as ambitious as any of the previous speculators'. He hoped to build extra houses to attract permanent staff and to make the land on which the hotel stood into a viable agricultural holding, geared to serve the hotel with fresh produce. With a commercial base thus established, Mike also envisaged the hotel becoming once again a focus for glen activities, with perhaps the eventual take-over of the concern by inhabitants of the glen on a co-operative basis. He looked to the Highlands and Islands Development Board to provide much of the initial funding, but found to his disappointment that their vision did not match his. As it turned out, he and the French financier had to go it alone.

'You can more or less sum up our ideas for the hotel itself by saying that we wanted to put back the fireplaces,' said Mike enigmatically.

Away with the hissing gas, the plastic fittings, all the hints of tasteless, creeping modernity, back to the warm glow in the fireplace, the honest heat of peat or birch logs, the casual but intimate service, the cosy snuggery bar – the real ethnic atmosphere of the West Highlands in its unregenerative charm.

But there were more pressing realities. Ironically, in a land deluged in water, the hotel's water supply – or lack of – was not part of the charm. When the burns dried up and the water table sank in the summer months, the hotel had to import fresh water by tanker and ration it out to guests and staff alike: so much to drink, so much to wash with, so much to flush the loos. And it seemed to be the last of these priorities which suffered first. The odours rising out back were formidable, as Monsieur Jean-Pierre might have said if he had stayed around for very long. But he had other interests, other commitments elsewhere and so was rarely seen about. When Mike mooted his idea of maybe a few animals around to supply fresh milk, Jean-Pierre said reputedly, 'Cows – here ? No I do not like zat.'

Debate ended. And end of Mike's dreams.

Looking round at what Mike and his family have managed to build up over seventeen years, the croft with its six acres of sweat, the ramshackle buildings, the holiday business, one is led to wonder whether he sees as much of a future here as he sees of a past. Is there anything in it to keep his children here? Both he and Bell pause a long time before answering the question.

'I think it really comes down to enablement. I mean, there's enough business here, enough money, enough work… but the whole depends on so many factors, so many other people, whether in effect the Forestry Commission, the hotel, the HIDB, the estate owners are all prepared to let efforts like this continue on the same terms, with leases, the use of the land. The business itself is perfectly viable, we've been here long enough to prove that… but in the end it really does depend on others enabling the thing to go on.'

As we talked, the evening drew in. Nobody moved to add a light to the room, so faces and bodily shapes gradually receded in the gloom, voices grew more spectral. Maybe when people know they are more or less invisible, they allow themselves to become more frank and open. People have to co-operate in this part of the world in order to thrive, but Mike felt they did so less than they used to. The creeping spirit of commercialism/materialism was permeating all layers of society.

'It used to be that a man would say "I'd like to build up a fine flock of sheep," and that consideration would govern whether or not, for instance, he sold or kept a particular ewe. But now he thinks first how much he might get for a beast at market, and that governs his decision regardless of how it affects the long term quality of his flock. Do you see what I mean ? I've always thought that if a man's first thought is 'I want a fine flock of sheep,' he will usually end up financially right as well – but people don't see it like this any more.'

We left just about midnight. The night was surprisingly light, there was no difficulty finding our way back down to the boat. We rowed back the short distance across the placid water, looking back at the receding light from the house. With all Mike's forebodings, one really had the impression of returning to a mainland from an island of dreams.

And what is it about such places as the glen that attracts those who actively seek to live a life devoid of the comforts or vanities of civilisation, and those who strive to express a creativity they believe can be released somehow once beyond the constraints of contemporary urban life? It was evident that most of the incomers to the glen could be classified into two categories, cowboys and dreamers, which were also gendered. The men shared backgrounds of practical experience with horses or boats: the women in painting or textiles. Tim, as aspiring writer, was the exception to the rule. The wildness of the area, its vastness, its remoteness, its pristine beauty, its very lack of the 'normal' trappings of modern life, its freedom from the petty demands of bourgeois life, its return to an elemental relationship with the realities of water, earth, weather – do these create a parallel sense of expansiveness, an encouragement to open one's inner self, give it space to explore and develop, a belief that one is in touch with the real 'real'? The answer can be yes or no depending on one's convictions. And of course the retreat to the wild is not exactly a new phenomenon, it can be traced back to the Romans and no doubt beyond. Yet the fact that the myth lives on, and compels people to act on it, suggests its power. Suggests too how it can overcome a daily experience which gives it the lie. For the effort needed just to exist in such places diverts energies needed for more visionary projects. The very distances and weather conditions impose often insurmountable obstacles.

Richie

There was a smallholding way up the glen road, which whenever we passed conjured up the aura of a little hell on earth – not the hell of fire and brimstone, but the hell of cold, mud-soaked hopelessness. Richie had a dream of a homestead rising from this bog, to be stocked with cattle and ponies, but his was an impossible battle against soil, climate, lack of capital. In order to make ends almost meet, he took on whatever extra work he could find in the glen – with the forestry or as a ghillie for neighbouring estates during the stalking season for which he would often set out on horseback. His wife too undertook an array of different work, and displayed a remarkably cheery attitude to what seemed a dour existence. Certainly, their children's main purpose seemed to be to quit the glen at the earliest opportunity. An incident which somehow epitomised Richie's fate was when his car self-combusted one day and burnt out: he was perhaps the sort of man that sort of accident befalls. Yet the defining image of Richie was one encountered from time to time when driving up the glen of an evening – he would be walking slowly home in the gloaming, leading his pony, just like the cowboy at the end of a long day on the trail. A weary, proud and quietly satisfied figure.

Yet Richie's was not the only tale of struggle against odds. To arrive in an area like the outer Highlands without a substantial financial cushion, is to be doomed before one starts. There is always the need to pay for repairs, extra fodder, petrol. We went through our savings in three years. Our new neighbours at the farm had no savings.

Tony and Miranda

One fine day we found Roddie and Peter had moved up the glen to 'more comfortable accommodation'. This was estate-speak for 'you two can't have the whole farmhouse and yard when we could let it out commercially'. Indeed there could be few houses less comfortable than the farmhouse, and by moving up the glen they would be nearer other friends and much nearer civilisation. But we were, selfishly, very sorry to see them go.

Yet it was not long before the farm had new tenants and we gained new neighbours with whom we became even closer than with Peter and Roddie. This was partly because Tony and Miranda were incomers too, struggling in their very different way to realise a vision in this difficult place. And struggle Tony and Miranda certainly did.

Tony was a forty something, ex-commando, abrasive true pioneer. He had started up and run an outward-bound trekking centre for Dr Barnardo's children on the loch immediately to the south. Miranda had come as a temporary housekeeper during her gap year after studying art in London. They seemed an unlikely couple; indeed Tony's friends had been astounded when he announced his marriage – he had been after all a convinced bachelor. And how could young Miranda give herself to life in a glen even more remote than ours? But marry they did and then Barnardos decided to pull the funding on the trekking centre. Thus it was that one rainy day, Miranda plus new-born baby Hugh, arrived by boat, followed by Tony driving fifteen reluctant ponies along the precipitous lochside path. For a couple with a baby, the farmhouse must have seemed basic beyond belief. It had water piped from the hill which like ours flowed erratically; no electricity at all, lighting was by oil lamps; no Rayburn, just an open range fireplace.

As they arrived in the winter and the pony-trekking business could not function until the spring, there was time for visiting to and fro across the river and time to become better acquainted. Once more or less settled in, Tony occupied himself with the ponies, endlessly mucking out the yard with military efficiency in rain, gale and snow, whilst Miranda battled with the deficiencies on the domestic front. The predominant images remain of Tony brandishing broom, cursing the weather and his fate at arriving at 'this trench' – or slumped in the chair by the dwindling fire behind the newspaper; and Miranda, with babe tucked under her arm, hustling around tending to fire and cooking, or endlessly washing baby gear in cold water. But for all the shared moans on the primitive conditions of our existence, there were occasions of merry fellowship over good meals, fits of laughter at Tony's fund of hilarious anecdotes, and even summer days of sunshine, playing with Hugh in the garden.

> *A wild day – sleet, wind, rain. Fixed goats' partition. Lina for New Year sherry and coffee. Tim set off for the Tomdoun shoot and returned soon after when he drove into a blizzard. Walked over to M's for tea through blinding rain. All very cosy there, first time in the pleasant sitting room, books, log fire and huge tea. Home with a book each: for me, L.Hill's gardening tome; for Tim one on Waterloo which he read aloud to me as I was weaving.*

To run a pony-trekking business from such a remote spot proved a logistical and emotional challenge. Tony had devised a unique holiday on horseback by offering one and two-week treks from coast to coast across the Highlands. A wonderful project, but one which involved endless negotiations with landowners for access, costly accommodation bookings, a substantial back-up organization, and enormous reserves of energy. And, initially, everything had to be run by Tony and Miranda themselves. We watched in admiration as they tried to make it work against all odds – and all odds there were. It seems at times that fate does declare against particular people or projects, and so it seemed for Tony and Miranda. Whatever could go wrong, did go wrong: the weather was appalling; people cancelled at the last minute; access was suddenly denied; a pony – or two – went lame; the back-up vehicle broke down; the bank refused a loan; Hugh went sick; it was incredible how they were beset with one disaster after another. And in fact it was only after they finally gave up on the glen and moved to a more amenable location that their fortunes changed for the better. But for two years we shared their struggles, which had the benefit for us of making ours seem manageable!

Ted and Jean

In contrast to the barrenness of bog which sucks one down to a dull and doomed existence, the sea leads outwards to the wider world from the confines of rocky hillsides. Maybe this creates a more optimistic outlook, encouraging greater success. Certainly one family of incomers from the sea proved adaptable enough in their efforts and were never defeated.

Ted had been a captain in the merchant navy. Subsequently, from a base in British Columbia where he had built a 70' sloop out of chicken wire and cement, he and his wife, Jean, four children and a cat, sailed back across the Atlantic. He had brought the boat to rest in the loch and casting about for a living, the family moved into the estate job now taken over by us. In addition, Ted chartered his boat for private trips in the summer months, contracted with a school to provide training exercises, and tried his hand at diving for scallops in the spring. This last venture, although profitable at times, was a risky business. With one of his sons controlling things from above, Ted would dive down to the loch bed in his wet suit, risking hypothermia as snow might be falling on the surface of the water above him. Boasting that they could 'live on the smell of an oily rag', they only ever kept one foot metaphorically on shore. The boat was always stocked and fuelled in readiness for departure should the urge take them.

For most of the time that we were in the glen, Ted's boat was moored in the inner loch. From here he and Jean would depart and to here they would at some unannounced time return. Except that is for one memorable time when their imminent arrival was relayed to us [how I can no longer recall] with an urgent request for assistance. The boat's motor had failed and Ted was coming into the loch under sail. To enter the inner loch meant negotiating a tight S channel between shallow sandbanks and rocks. It was difficult enough rowing a dinghy through; we were aghast at how Ted could possibly get 70' of ferro concrete through. There was not time to dither however; we were instructed to get the dinghy out to the mooring and await orders. Handling boats did not come naturally to us, and our experience to date had not prepared us for keeping cool as Ted's huge vessel hove into view. We were so transfixed watching it approaching the narrows at some speed, that we had not noticed the screws fixing the outboard to the dinghy had become loose and, as Ted was miraculously piloting round the sandbanks, we were suddenly spinning in uncontrollable circles round the mooring as one side of the motor mounting gave way. Ted's boat was almost upon us and he was hollering and preparing to throw us a line to catch as Tim desperately struggled to

get the outboard back on its mounting. The panic probably prevented us turning tail as we faced from our miniscule dinghy the might of the bow bearing down on us. Somehow the outboard was attached, our manic spinning steadied and I caught the flying rope from Ted and tied it to the mooring buoy. Just in time. Tim turned the dinghy from under the towering hull which was still travelling at speed and, virtually scraping sides, we bounced away over the swell. At least it wasn't blowing a gale that day.

In spite of Ted's kind offers to teach us to sail later on, we thought we would be happy enough to improve our mastery of the outboard and oars before attempting any sailing experiences.

Jean, while also being an experienced sailor, was a fine artist. When they left the estate, they moved up the glen and established themselves among the people on the neighbouring estate. Here, Jean ran an art class, and spent time when the children were away at school in roaming the hills sketching. Yet, in time, even they left the glen; when Ted finally sold the boat, they turned their energies to developing Jean's talent into a successful line of Highland prints and moved away.

The James' hotel and holiday aspirations; Tony and Miranda's pony-trekking venture; Ted's sailing enterprises run from the loch; Richie's dream of a homestead rising from the bog – pioneers all, men able and strong, but whose dreams were affected by the very elements which attract. The glen was the edge of the world, the whiff of the last frontier, where a man's a man for a' that. Many of the men had a service background. When their careers in army or navy were closed down by age or other circumstance, they looked for another physical challenge to engage their restlessness. They tended to look boyish, and to think and act in youthful, adventurous terms. They relished the open skies, the earth or a boat deck beneath their feet, a good strong breeze on their face, and no need to carry a watch.

Creativity too needs time, and in this environment time is taken up entirely with survival. Creativity also needs stimulation not just from scenery but from the responses of others, from a viewer, a reader, an outlet. The space to practise one's craft is limited by cramped living quarters, and the time prised out of the day's essential duties is lost to journeys to markets or even to the post – for Hilary, down the loch, trying to run an original knitwear business, getting to the post entailed a 40 minute crossing of the loch, weather permitting. For Hilary also success eventually meant a departure from the wild.

And, so, we too found our dreams challenged by reality. Those early visions were not realisable within the context here of place and time. What emerged however was a new vision, growing out of the particularity of this place, this time, these people. Not a vision imported and imposed upon a romantic preconception, but a re-vision, a deepening awareness of an active actuality. An insight perhaps rather than the other-worldly suggestion of 'vision', an insight into the richness of what was all around us, which as the dreams faded became an even greater source of wonder and admiration.

Endings

Crack-Up – Tim's Last Stalk

The snow lay soft and deep and dazzling in the gullies, smothering the stones, deceptive in its blanketing. The weather had forced the deer down to the lower levels so that it seemed a good chance to bring in the last beasts needed for the year's quota. He started along the drive from which he could spy groups of hinds on the nearest slopes. Circling round the knollies into dead ground, he approached them from below. His first attempt was clumsy, for when he reached the crest of the first hump, expecting to get a shot, he found that the deer had moved, crossing the broken line of the wall onto higher ground. This meant that he had to climb higher again, working up the adjacent small corrie to reach a new vantage point. Here the winds had blown the snow into deeper drifts, and though he only had to climb about forty feet, it became a marathon effort. At every other step he fell, either into a trough of snow up to his waist, or his boot slid off a hidden rock, jarring his ankle. He began to curse: the gods were against him; the elements were malevolent. Each time he stumbled, the snow packed up inside his sleeves, down his neck, into his boots, and worst of all down the muzzle of the rifle, which he had taken out of its cover at the first anticipation of a shot. The leather muzzle-cover had frayed and pushed up uselessly past the end of the barrel. In his ignorance he was not sure how much snow stuffed down the barrel would cause catastrophe if a bullet were fired. He could imagine the barrel splitting and peeling back like a banana skin, leaving him with a sooty face and no eyebrows.

His spastic scramble up the puny hill was so laboured he was doubtful the deer would still be waiting to be shot at by the time he got into position. With every stumble and flounder he became more exhausted and pathetically furious. When he reached the shoulder of the ridge and flopped down on his stomach, he was grateful to see the deer still in the hollow, placidly pawing away at the snow to reach the heather underneath. Keeping out of sight he prepared the rifle, winking the fresh snow out of the muzzle and easing a round up the spout as quietly as possible, as even the click of a rifle bolt carried a distance in that atmosphere. He eased forward, wiped the condensation off the telescopic sight and aimed carefully at the nearest suitable hind. He waited for his breathing to slow down before feeling steady enough to take a shot. The deer were still oblivious. He squeezed the trigger. The shot reverberated around the corrie. The deer looked up. But none of them moved. Worse, none of them fell down. His target unscathed. One or two of the hinds resumed foraging. They had not spotted him, so were unsure where the noise had come from. So, obligingly, they waited. He swore and hurried to reload. Too fast – the spent cartridge jammed in the breech. He wrenched at the bolt, regardless of the giveaway noise. Rammed in another round and took aim at the same hind. He fired again – and missed again. It was scarcely believable. Was this some kind of super-beast? At length the deer decided that if it was not particularly dangerous here it was getting rather too noisy, and in good order they drifted uphill, out of sight over the next rise. His opportunity was gone.

    Later he discovered from the local gunsmith that the rifling in the gun barrel had gone, so he had little chance of hitting anything he aimed at smaller than a mountain side. But now he could only feel his total incompetence and inadequacy. His body shook with sobs of frustration and exhaustion. He lay with his face in the snow, the dampness seeping through his clothes, his will gone, utterly spent, enveloped in a child's helplessness, worked out in a tantrum of impotent rage.

That was one version of the end.

Endings

And this is another:

After three years in the glen our lives had settled into familiar routines. There were frequent mishaps, of course, but on the whole we were coping and feeling at home. Yet what occurred in that third summer was a challenge too far. Tim had started suffering from extreme debilitation and intense headaches. He was finally diagnosed with renal failure and his condition deteriorated rapidly. Seventy miles from a hospital, at the end of a single track road which could be blocked for days in winter, and with limited facilities at the end of it needing regular physical attention – this was no place in which to be chronically ill. Nor was it possible for us to stay in a tied house when Tim could no longer do the job. We had to go. The laird was sympathetic and did not press us to leave whilst we tried to re-organize our next move, but, being quite unfamiliar with serious illness and medical matters, and stunned by the gradual realization of what was happening, we moved slowly. Financially too we could hardly do otherwise. Our limited capital had gone into our self-sufficiency ventures which ironically were only now bearing fruit. We stayed on in the glen through the following winter and the dream became a nightmare.

> *To Inverness. Tim low today – consultant's missive re-machine treatment, and his illness generally, depressing him. His weakness infuriates and humiliates him. Prospect of buying 'The Firs' also doomed – no money possible except via Building Societies and we're out of the running there. Deep disappointment. Back home in howling blizzard – snow drifting and tracks gone; very relieved to get home – almost skidded into the burn at the front door! Chicken soup and bed.*
>
> *Sat and talked of future plans all evening. Tim's sprits very low – how else in the circumstances. When he was so fit, to*

realise how very ill he is is shocking. However much one jokes, or makes light of it all, the reality is horribly apparent these days.

When we eventually left, it was with relief mixed with deep sadness. We had come so innocently – so ignorantly – and had, with help of new friends, met challenges we had never imagined we could face. It had been an 'adventure' in every sense and we felt we had 'arrived'. It had tested our individual strengths, our adaptability, our relationship. We had learnt a range of new skills, acquired new knowledge, gained an insight into a world on the brink of change.

The glen encompassed a social history rare in mid twentieth century Britain. The way of life still adhered to at the lodge stretched back to the late nineteenth century. Indeed the traditional attitudes and assumptions of the lairds and lodge staff were in many respects feudal, based on loyalty, service and provision of life's necessities in kind not cash. The lives of some of our crofting neighbours looked back through generations of unbroken custom to much earlier centuries. This was a different concept of time. Here the key markers of twentieth century life – petrol and motors on cars and boats – existed alongside live memories of horses and oars. Radio and TV were unobtainable at our end of the glen, and electricity and the phone [with its radio link] were unreliable. Oil lamps and candles were necessities not nostalgia. When TV did reach the hamlet halfway up the glen, it brought an abrupt end to evening socialising between the houses there. The piles of newspapers and magazines shrank, the knitting bags were put aside as the flickering screens took over. And on the hills, the finely laid and drained paths, rigorously maintained in former years by a sizeable resident workforce, were falling into disrepair and soon became broken up with the introduction of snowcats and snowmobiles. We were privileged to live in this place at a watershed in its history: we were in time to get a genuine sense of that former world, its smells, its

Endings

touch, its taste through existing traditions and oral renditions, not just a glimpse through sepia prints. And we saw how it all faded away as more sophisticated machinery and technologies arrived, and our elderly friends died. More comfort and convenience, of course, but no gain without loss!

But for us that adventure was over and a new one was beginning. Here too lay undreamt-of challenges waiting for us, but that of course is another story…